ADVENTURE CARAVANNING WITH DOGS

DOG ON THE RHINE

JACQUELINE MARY LAMBERT

Copyright & Disclaimer

Contact:

Facebook:@JacquelineLambertAuthor

Amazon:www.amazon.com/author/jacquelinelambert

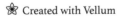 Created with Vellum

From Rat Race to Road Trip

Adventure Caravanning With Dogs

Dog on the Rhine

Jacqueline Lambert

Mum – When we lost you, the whole world lost a little sparkle.

PROLOGUE

A small, black dog ran back to a caravan across a short
expanse of grass.
Its owners were evicted.

...

They couldn't wait to get back to the Continent. There, they
had never been subjected to such nonsense.
Until they got to Austria...

INTRODUCTION

"You honestly can't think of a better way to spend these moments? This is your life. And it's ending one minute at a time." - Tyler Durden in the movie Fight Club.

We're "That couple with four dogs." Otherwise known as Jackie and Mark Lambert, we are two fifty-somethings who accidentally bought our first caravan after being made redundant. We called her 'Kismet' which means 'Fate'.

Celebrating our caravan purchase, we got a little tipsy and hatched a plan to rent out our house, sell most of our possessions and tour full-time, calling it 'early retirement.' Unlike most people, however, once we were sober, that is exactly what we did.

'Dog on the Rhine' is the true story of our second year on wheels with Kismet and 'Big Blue' – our trusty tow vehicle (and toy box) - a Hyundai iLoad panel van, pictured here at Wasser Schloss Podelwitz, near Colditz in Germany.

Accompanied by our four cuddly Cavapoos, Kai, Rosie, Ruby and Lani, we got a bit more adventurous in our second year and crossed from France into Germany before going for a brief bark around Bohemia and the Balkans *(The Czech Republic, Slovenia and Croatia.)* We were evicted from Austria but stopped for some R&R in Italy and, lest we mislead you into thinking that that Livin' the Dream is all sunshine and cornflakes, we returned to the UK to be confronted by a huge Fidose of Reality.

Dog on the Rhine is the second book in the 'Adventure Caravanning with Dogs' series and is the follow up to 'Year 1 - Fur Babies in France – From Wage Slaves to living the Dream'.

The Fab Four. From Left to Right; Lani, Ruby, Rosie and Kai at Festung Königstein in the Saxon Swiss National Park, Germany.

1

MEET THE JOBSWORTHS

"Jobsworth – an official who upholds petty rules even at the expense of humanity or common sense."

The Wife checked in. "We're new to the job. We opened today but we've been here for a couple of days. It's been AWFUL. It took us A DAY to clean the shower blocks!" She rolled her eyes to convey that she was the sole combatant in a war against the thorough incompetence of EVERYONE IN THE WHOLE WORLD. "The card machine is really slow. I don't know how to process your 'One Night Free' voucher. I'll leave that to The Boss."

There were four of them. They all looked the same. Fat. Grey. Belligerent. Their faces looked like the wind had changed during a gurning competition at a Les Dawson Lookalike Convention.

With a smile, The Wife said that she didn't mind waiting. She was happy. It was sunny. The birds were singing and Spring was on its way. She was on holiday, so it was no problem to hang around until someone was able to serve her. She passed the time empathising with The Jobsworth at the insurmountable challenges that presented themselves in the dream lifestyle so carefully chosen by a Site Warden. She thought to herself that they could always try what The Husband and Wife used to do for a living. The Wife was not sure that they would last an hour.

"Welcome! We hope that you enjoy your stay." Oooops. That was me who said that. The Wife. Not our hosts. But to give them their due, they were very, very stressed. And offering a warm welcome to a paying guest was clearly not in the job description.

...

During their stay, The Husband and Wife tried to be pleasant and passed the time of day whenever they saw A Jobsworth around the site. "Hi! How are you today?" they would ask cheerily. "You wouldn't BELIEVE the amount of leaves we've had to clear up!" The Jobsworths would complain by way of reply. The Husband and Wife mentioned in passing that the internet was not very good. "Don't talk to US about internet. We can't get internet and IMAGINE trying to do OUR job without THAT!"

"I need some change for the dryer. We have a very sick puppy and rather a lot of laundry to dry..." Those eyes rolled again although surprisingly, not at The Wife; "They DIDN'T LEAVE US A FLOAT!" The implied incompetence of the entire world again. She rummaged through the till, left the office, went to get some bags of change, emptied her handbag and gave The Wife a fiver's worth of £1 coins. The Wife thanked her profusely for going the extra mile to help. The Wife assured her that she hadn't minded the wait at all. The Wife was just worried about the dog.

The Husband carried the dog as he went to collect the

laundry from the dryer so as not to leave it on its own. He was worried that it might bark and they would get a complaint. The Wife was out walking the other dogs. The Husband carried the dog because the dog was too poorly to walk. The poorly dog pooped down The Husband's side. He put down the dog, who continued to squat. Even before he had chance to reach for a poo bag, a Jobsworth materialised. "That dog should be on a lead! And I hope you're going to clear THAT up! And you're NOT taking that dog into the showers!" A man with liquid poo sliding down his shirt and shorts reeled under the barrage.

Compassion and humanity? Empathy – or assistance in an obviously difficult and upsetting situation? These are not within the emotional repertoire of A Jobsworth. If a stick becomes available, A Jobsworth is honour-bound to beat their victim with it as hard as they can and, if the opportunity presents, kick them while they're down for good measure.

The Husband and Wife were quite proud of their portable washing machine. Their caravan, Kismet, also had her own onboard shower. The Husband and Wife often joked that the caravan shower was used almost exclusively by the dogs. The Husband and Wife speculated that they had more facilities than most guests with young children or those using the incontinence products for which disposal facilities were provided on site.

However, that didn't stop The Jobsworths from making the accusation that 'a couple' had rung The Environmental Health because The Husband had been seen washing soiled items in the laundry. Now let me see, Sherlock but it seemed odd that The Jobsworth knew that it was 'a couple' rather than just 'someone' who had called Environmental Health. And, Watson, there were hardly any other guests on site.

The only witness was The Jobsworth who had seen The Husband in the laundry, using the dryer.

But here we have another typical behaviour of The Jobsworth. MUSTETS – or 'Making Up Stuff To Exaggerate The Seriousness.' Or in the common parlance, fibbing.

A couple of days later, a small black dog ran back to a caravan across a short expanse of grass. The short expanse was an area that required dogs to be on leads. The dog had run from The Husband, in a field where leads were not required, directly back to The Wife in the caravan. On the way, it did not stop or cause nuisance. It did not pass 'Go' nor collect £200. It just moved to the caravan. Directly to the caravan. Crossing five yards where it should have been on a lead. The dog didn't think of that. It just wanted its breakfast.

"Dogs should be on a lead. A SHORT LEAD!" The Jobsworth growled at The Wife through the awning and stomped off before The Wife could answer.

"I have just been told off!" The Wife told The Husband when he got back with the other dogs, all on their leads, thirty seconds later. The Husband went to explain to The Jobsworth what had happened. "The dogs have been on the lead on site the whole time we have been here. Lani just ran back to the caravan to get her breakfast. Let's be reasonable here. It's a one-off and it's a couple of yards. She hasn't caused a problem." The Jobsworth didn't reply. She just turned her back on The Husband and stalked off. "Don't walk away from me when I'm talking to you! That's really rude!" The Husband said to The Jobsworth, who ignored him completely and wobbled on her way.

"It is UNACCEPTABLE to raise your voice to a member of staff!" the husband of The Jobsworth growled at The Wife through the awning. The Big Boss sent to pick on The

Woman. "If it happens again, you will be asked to leave." He stomped off before The Wife could answer.

"I have just been told off!" The Wife told The Husband when he came back from the loo. The Husband said to The Wife that he would go to explain and calm the situation. "I'm going to give them a piece of my mind!" were his exact words. "I will not be spoken to like that. AND there is no soap in the toilets."

The Wife just hid. She later managed to piece together a dialogue that seemed to have gone along the lines of The Jobsworth telling The Husband to leave the site for raising his voice and The Husband saying that since they refused to refund the site fee, he would not be moving anywhere and that there was no excuse for being rude to customers and then playing the "Don't raise your voice or we'll kick you out" card.

The Wife cried. Never one to overreact, she was sure that she and The Husband would now be black balled at every campsite in the whole of the United Kingdom, if not The Universe.

The Husband and The Wife had been very worried about their Fur Family for days. Having four sick dogs in a caravan had not been fun and one of the puppies had been so ill that they had thought that they were going to lose her. She had lost one eighth of her body weight and been kept in by the vet because she needed intravenous fluids. Being constantly picked on by petty-minded Jobsworths was really not what The Husband and Wife needed.

Finally, The Jobsworths offered a refund for the remainder of the week and The Husband and Wife agreed to move. It was a shame, as it was a lovely site overlooking a lake and had a nice, dry dog walk close by. But, The Husband and Wife didn't want to be glared at for the rest of their stay by the grumpy, old gits running it. The Husband and Wife had tried to choose a quiet and relaxed lifestyle; they did not want to be constantly looking over their shoulders and worrying about what they would be told off for next.

The Husband and Wife lodged a complaint with the club who ran the site. They suggested that since The Jobsworths were in a public-facing role, they might benefit from training in proportionate response and how to speak to their guests without making them feel like they were unwelcome trespassers on The Jobsworths' own private estate, who should constantly be ordered around like 6-year-old imbeciles short of some serious time on the naughty step.

A nice man followed up the complaint and very pleasantly told The Husband and Wife that The Jobsworths' version of the story had been different from theirs but apologised if there had been any offence. The Husband and Wife said that they were not surprised that the stories were different.

While they didn't say so, The Husband and Wife had already established The Jobsworths' willingness to resort to MUSTETS. And rude officials always fall back on "We will not tolerate abuse!" Unless, of course, they are the ones giving it.

Instead, The Husband and Wife conceded that they were clearly Public Enemy No1. The nice man laughed.

...

A small, black dog ran back to a caravan across a short expanse of grass.

The dog caused no nuisance. Other than the outbreak of

World War III. The dog's owners were evicted from the site and were very upset. They felt they had not really done anything wrong and had to spend a lovely, sunny day packing up and moving to another site, 100 miles away from a 94-year-old parent, with whom they had come to spend time after being abroad for 3-months. The 94-year-old parent was housebound. She didn't get the lunch out that she was so looking forward to. She didn't have the company that she had been promised for the week, her shopping was not done and her garden was not tidied.

No doubt The Jobsworths were also upset, because they had a complaint lodged to their superiors in their very first week in the job. Undoubtedly, they would think that they had done nothing wrong, since their style of Management and Customer Care was carefully modelled on issuing diktats over their fiefdom, like all-powerful Uber Führers. It is a tried and tested system. It worked for Adolf. For a short while, at least.

And there you have the anatomy of a completely avoidable Lose : Lose situation. The Perfect Storm in a Teacup.

But that is how wars start!

Postscript

<A passage of time. Mostly on the M3.>

The Husband and Wife arrived at Verwood, a site near the New Forest.

"Welcome!" said The Warden, greeting The Wife as she walked up the path, even before she had reached Reception. "I don't know how to process your 'One Night Free' voucher, but I'll get my wife to sort it." It was dealt with in short order and then The Warden said, "I'll show you to your pitch!" He helped The Husband and Wife to manoeuvre and level and said "Have a great stay. If there's anything else you need, you know where I am!"

No complaints, moans or gripes about the world being against him. Just a bit of customer focus. That seemed a bit more like it!

And since this was The Husband and Wife's second stay at Verwood, The Warden just happened to mention in passing that he was delighted to see them back again because they were "Model guests."

Now who would have thought that?

VACATIONING IN VERWOOD

The Official Start of Spring & Our Caravanniversary!

While often, we give them names and even attribute person-alities, I think that most people love their caravans and motorhomes not because of what they are, but because of what they represent; freedom.

Jobsworths aside, it was great to be back on wheels. It was officially Spring. The sea temperature had just crawled up to 10.2°C so it was definitely The Windsurfing Season. *(We work on the principle that we can windsurf so long as SOMETHING – either the air temperature or water temperature – is in double figures.)* 10.2°C left us with no excuse...

A full, pink moon brought us high tides at Mudeford to coincide with 14mph westerly winds and some sunshine. It was time to squeeze the lithe and muscular skiing body (which was well hidden under the insulation layer of stodgy, mountain energy food) into that wetsuit.

Sandwiches made. Van loaded. Bikini on. Remembered to put towel and spare undies in a bag (always grim forgetting your dry undies). Then the wind forecast downgraded itself to 6mph.

Welcome to the Windsurfing Season!

...

Our little Ruby was improving. We were unsure whether her illness had been caused by an adverse reaction to the mandatory tapeworm treatment administered prior to our return to the UK, or an infection picked up in the dog area of a French Aire. Being a Princess, she was feeling a little bit sorry for herself. She needed lots of love!

But the retired, travelling person always has things to do. Besides nursing Ruby, Mark optimised the racking in the van in preparation for our next European trip. I sold all the things that we had bought for our first trip and had never used (i.e. most of them!) And more importantly, we treated ourselves to an Al Fresco fry up. With proper sausages, bacon and a Bury black pudding.

We spent lots of time walking in the bluebell woods next to the campsite. The scent was AMAZING. Well aware that Mark is a soft touch, Ruby was at the stage of recovery which required frequent cuddles and being carried on walks because she was still just so POORLY! Although, every now and again, Princess did forget that she was ill and if we put her down, she attacked Lani or went for a chase along the path...

We embarked on a progress around the UK to visit friends and family. "You can't leave! You're part of the furniture - and you're model campers!" We had stayed at Verwood for seventeen days. We would miss the bluebells, the lovely Wardens and our neighbours; Helen with her King Charles Spaniel and William the collie.

"Drive safely!" everyone shouted as they waved us off. The Sat Nav took us on a long and winding road that wiggled through picture-perfect villages with names that would make fabulous characters in a Miss Marple 'Who-dunnit?!' – Kingsbury Episcopi, Staple Fitzpaine and the twins; Shepton- and Hatch Beauchamp.

We braved the mud in Lancashire once again before returning to the south coast, where we evicted ourselves from a campsite! We were supposed to stay at a small, privately-owned site affiliated to one of the main clubs, but the lady owner was so grumpy on arrival that we left immediately.

The moment we got there, we were told off for arriving earlier than we had said. We apologised but explained that we had been forced to estimate our journey time for a 300-mile drive with a caravan in unpredictable May Bank Holiday traffic. We said that we didn't mind waiting if it was inconvenient for her.

Then, she informed us that the dogs were not allowed to pee or poo anywhere, even if we picked it up. We were being charged an extra £4 per night for the pups because there was a 'dog area' - a corner of the field the size of a postage stamp, which was the only place where the dogs were allowed to relieve themselves.

It prompted in our mind several questions;

1. Can canines distinguish between one part of a field and another?
2. Can some site wardens not even bring themselves to say 'Hello' before moaning at their guests?
3. Why advertise yourself as dog-friendly when you are quite patently not?

After seven hours on the road, we were quite simply not in the mood. We asked for our money back before we had even entered the gate, then we left.

We returned to Verwood, where we knew that we would be made welcome. The Verwood site has facilities - and we worked out that it was in fact CHEAPER than Mrs McWelcome's field next to the main road and under the flight path of Bournemouth Airport. And even when we had been in residence for a couple of hours, no-one had moaned at us. Hurrah!

6th May - The old, paper £5 note went out of circulation. That is irrelevant but I just thought that I would mention it, since I have a loosely currency-related subject to tackle.

Mark likes to be tidy. This has resulted in a number of very Magical Markie Moments over the years. This is because Mark has no filter on his need to clear the decks. Anything can quite literally be found anywhere once he has tidied up – and he LOVES chucking stuff away...

On returning from holiday, he would immediately shred all redundant paperwork. Once, this meant that along with all our used tickets and itineraries, he also shredded all of our uncashed travellers' cheques. "It's OK" I optimised (my verb for being stupidly optimistic.) "We still have the sheet with all the travellers' cheque number on it!" I knew instantly from the look on his face; he had shredded that too.

So, I was not altogether surprised when he uttered an oath and recovered several pieces of a torn cheque from the bin in the caravan, laid them out on the table and asked me "Do you think the bank will accept this?"

The ripped cheque was our refund from the site from which we had just evicted ourselves. "I thought she just gave us back our own deposit cheque..." Said Magic Markie in mitigation. I was dubious, but certainly rated our chances with the bank as better than trying to get a replacement cheque out of Mrs McWelcome!

To the absolute credit of Barclays Bank, they came up trumps on both occasions. They found all the numbers of our unused, shredded travellers' cheques and refunded them. Then, when we explained what had happened with the deposit cheque, the cashier did grin, but allowed us to pay the sellotaped-together pieces of cheque into our account, thus avoiding the need for any further contact with the hatchet-faced Mrs McW.

7th May - We moved from Verwood to Salisbury and were delighted to be greeted by the lovely Steve, who had helped us out so kindly on our Maiden Voyage last year. Strangely, he remembered us; the incompetent pair who had turned up in a blue van with surf boards strapped to the roof, four dogs and a 7.3m caravan, which they had owned for less than half an hour and had no idea how to pitch...

Unfortunately, within moments of arriving, Mark had bent his pole. I had taken the pups for a run over the iron age fort at Old Sarum while Mark set up. I seem to remember suggesting that he postponed his erection until tomorrow, when he would be less likely to suffer from big bursts of wind. Mark being Mark, however, he insisted on putting up the awning. As a windsurfer, he should know that 25mph is a Force 6 - and not to be trifled with when trying to maintain control of a large expanse of canvas.

As I returned from walking the pooches, he greeted me with "There is good news and bad news... The good news is that the caravan is not damaged." And the bad news - "The awning is torn and a couple of the junction poles now need welding..."

Mysteriously, our dealer seemed to think that the

awning could be repaired under warranty. However, this was the only good news that we received from the dealer when our caravan went in for its first service.

10th **May** - AND – On this day in history...

We had been caravan owners for a whole year and caravan dwellers for 11 months and loving it. Let's just say; ROLLIN' ROCKS!

3

OPERATION OVERLOAD

*A Caravan Catastrophe, a Delayed Departure & some
Emergency Extinguishing*

We were on the way out of the door because we had just
received a phone call; "Your caravan is ready to collect from
its service."

The second phone call, ten minutes later, informed us
"Your caravan is unfit to drive."

The word "axle" was mentioned, as were the words "it is
your fault and not covered under warranty."

That was the bad news. Along with "And now you are
homeless!" of course. Since our caravan, Kismet, is our main
residence.

The good news was that at least the water ingress
problem had been solved.

The caravan had flooded twice when towed in the rain.
The dealer had put this down to "a one-off" – even when it
happened the second time.

It turned out that the source of the leak was a huge hole
in the offside wheel box. A huge hole that Mark had spotted

while lying on his back in a field, but which the dealer had failed to find when they "had it up on the ramp and went over it with a fine toothcomb" during the three days that they had spent searching for the cause of the first flood at the end of last year.

The huge hole had been caused by the tyre rubbing against the wheel box because the spreader arms on our 2-year-old caravan's axle had collapsed. A problem which the dealer told us they had never heard of before, although they were resolutely sure that it was our fault and had been caused by us overloading the caravan.

Overloading is a serious accusation to make; to do so is to break the law. And they were levelling this accusation at us! We, who tow with a panel van to carry anything heavy. We, who had a spreadsheet to prove that we had weighed every single item that we kept in the caravan; even the teaspoons...

The dealer's evidence against us on the overloading front initially centred around the caravan feeling "heavy to push around the yard."

"Friction on a wheel is the principle behind a braking system!" I suggested, to explain the perceived 'heaviness'. The dealer's chief engineer poo pooh-ed my idiotic proposal. I am female, after all, which fully negates that fluffy, pink Honours-degree-in-science thingy that I was awarded for turning up and looking pretty. I held back from suggesting that he try to push his car around the yard with the handbrake on to see if that "felt heavy". Logic was clearly not going to win the day.

A brief internet search quickly highlighted a widespread axle problem. However, as you do in these situations, we braced for the worst; a long time to fix and lots of zeros on the bill.

We agreed to pay upfront to expedite the repair and argue about the accusations and warranty afterwards. We had heard of warranty cases dragging on for months and we had a ferry booked. In the end, our arguments were fairly compelling, it seems, since after an initial refusal, we were grudgingly refunded for the parts and labour to replace the axle and wheel box.

Even so, we had to postpone our trip to Europe. We lost deposits on a couple of campsites that we had pre-booked, missed a rendezvous with friends and had no accommodation for the National Watersports Festival, for which we were volunteers.

Since we had let out our home to fund our travels, another consequence of the month that it took to repair our axle was a sudden plague which began to spread across the whole of England. A homeless couple with four dogs began to buzz around the countryside like a swarm of wasps. They descended on the floors, sofas and spare rooms of unsuspecting friends and family to make their nests for indeterminate periods of time; usually until they felt that their welcome had waned and they were forced to set out with their Queen to colonise fresh territory...

...

As part of the spreading of the burden of our homelessness, we headed back up north on an extra visit to see my Dad. We took Dad out to a country café for a nice, quiet bacon butty and a brew. Dad is a very laid-back man who objects to only two things in life; dogs and having his photo taken.

I do test my beloved parent. As an experiment, I once sent him a Christmas card featuring a festive picture of

Rosie, wondering how he would strike a balance between dog and daughter. I visited to find the rear of the card displayed on his mantelpiece. He had turned the picture towards the wall because it had a dog on it, but was displaying the card in pride of place since it was from his daughter. A stroke of genius in the art of compromise!

However, suffice to say that he was not at all chuffed at being served his coffee in a doggie mug, particularly in combination with me trying to shove a camera lens in his face. I was attempting to get a shot of him drinking from it to chortle over later with Ant Kath. Kath was puppy-sitting to save Dad from the trauma of being out with four 'unmentionables'; the only name by which he can bear to refer to our fur family.

No sooner had we been served our bacon butties than the shout went up; "FIRE!" A Land Rover, which had just pulled up in the car park, was ablaze. You always think you will be cool in a crisis, but everyone immediately launched into a flap – apart from the Land Rover's lady owner, who simply looked resigned, abandoned her vehicle and strode purposefully into the café to get herself a cup of tea.

I made my first ever 999 call, since nobody else had a phone and were, in any case, involved in a frenzied search for fire extinguishers. We had one in the back of the van – it is compulsory to carry one while driving in France. We acted quickly; after we auspiciously moved our van well away from the flaming Land Rover...

"Don't put yourselves in danger" I murmured ineffectually as someone tried to extinguish the flames with a dog bowl. Then I found my voice. "Come away – she might blow..." I yelled dramatically. She didn't. And we found an extinguisher. Then we joined the lady owner for a brew, during which she explained her look of resignation.

"We've just come back from Coniston." She said. "We were meant to do a swim tomorrow, but it was cancelled. The campsite was like a river. And now this. Well, it can only get better..."

Ah, that's the spirit. A bit of Northern optimism.

I soon needed to summon all of my Northern optimism. We called our dealer, who had by now had caravan Kismet in for repairs for a month, in the full knowledge that this meant that we were homeless all the while. We were expecting to collect her that Friday, so we thought that we would check to see how things were progressing. Although the work was scheduled, they told us that they didn't even have the part! No-one had thought to chase it up. "It won't be ready on Friday." they informed us cheerily. They also told us equally confidently that they couldn't tell us where the part was, when they were going to get it or when the caravan would be ready.

We had already had to delay our early June departure to the end of the month. We had left a margin as we are 'ye of little faith' (with good reason, it seemed) but it looked like we wouldn't be going then either.

Delighted did not even come close!

...

G Day – GO DAY! Our Invasion of Normandy.

I am an even-tempered person; always keen to find equitable solutions without resorting to conflict. "Lose your temper. Lose the argument" is my father's mantra on this subject and mostly, I agree. However, experience has taught me that sometimes, a well-timed tantrum can pay dividends. I deployed one over the phone to the dealer. Miraculously, the axle was found; it was couriered over; it was fitted

– and we DID get Kismet back on Friday, in good time to catch our ferry to France.

And so, we departed the fair shores of Blighty from Poole to Cherbourg; nearly a month late; in torrential rain; with both a new axle and a new sense of optimism that the caravan would no longer flood – and the earnest hope that in the next few months, it would not just fall apart like a clown car, somewhere in the middle of Europe.

4

FANDANGLES IN FRANCE – HIGH DRAMA ON THE HIGH SEAS!

An 'Optimism' Of Octogenarian Windsurfers Requires Rescue

Last Wednesday, it was Britain's hottest day since the heatwave of 1976. At 06:30, as we departed for the ferry, it rained. A lot. On the ferry it rained. A lot. And en route; a lot. We seemed to have exported British rain to Brittany, but at least it was exotic rain; rain with roulade rather than roast beef.

Kai had been unsettled by the journey and would agree to eat only when spoon fed. We had arrived in Penthièvre, on our annual pilgrimage to take to the seas with a windsurfing club for veterans. Holidaying with people who are mostly several decades your senior might not be the first choice for many, however these are among the most inspiring people that I have ever met. Their incredible lust for life remains undimmed by age. We are also grateful to them for the ideas that they gave us for our choice of lifestyle. Wandering Europe in their caravans and motorhomes is how many of them have chosen to spend their golden years.

I took the pups for their long-awaited walk on the beach and through the adjacent forest. The scent of pine took me straight back; not just to previous, happy times in Penthièvre. The aroma was as strong and heady as the patchouli oil with which we used to douse ourselves when we all dressed up as hippies in that legendary heatwave of 1976!

Then the rain abated and summer suddenly arrived. We all got quite excited about the wind forecast. I got as far as putting my sail, board and mast on the grass. "I'll just walk down to the shore and see what the wind is like" said Mark. He came back with the verdict "There's NOTHING!" he said. "You're joking!" I was incredulous. "There is more wind here by the caravan than down on the shore!"

I sought to verify his assertion by going to the beach to stand and rub my chin amid a scatter of boards, sails and wetsuit-clad personages, in true windsurfing fashion. "It was forecast to be 14-knots!" we admonished Reality. "The collective noun for a group of windsurfers should be 'An Optimism.'" I ventured. Several windsurfers on the beach chuckled with resigned recognition.

Mark and I opted for Pups on SUPs as an alternative and made an attempt to visit the Brussels Spruits, the Dutch family whom we had met last year. They were pitched at the far end of the campsite and looked surprised at the oceanic assault by two Stand Up Paddleboards (SUPs), carrying four dogs clad in colourful life jackets and powered by two pasty English paddlers. Ever the perfect hostess, Margaret didn't bat an eyelid when four wet dogs leapt from their Paddle-boards and ran straight across her beach blanket, immediately covering it with sand. Unruffled, she dismissed our apologies, shook out the blanket and rustled up four frothy coffees and four plates of delicious madeira cake, soaked with juicy, bittersweet, maraschino cherries.

We chatted and caught up with family news – new arrivals and sad departures; the last making us ever more sure that life is for living. Their gorgeous grand-daughter, whom we had met last year, had been spotted as a model. They showed us her picture in a magazine and told us that she was visiting Paris and Tokyo, although in between, she was busy finishing school and being a champion at hockey. Not bad at 17!

As we paddled back, we spotted The Optimism strung right across the bay to Carnac. Everyone was pumping their sails *(moving them backwards and forwards in a slightly circular motion; a technique to propel your board forward when there is no wind.)* It looked like hard work – it was nearly 30ºC and the sea was like a mirror. I went for a cooling swim and it felt like being in a massive infinity pool. Quiberon bay looked like a huge bolt of silk, rolled out its full length and shimmering blue and gold into the distance.

"Can I borrow your Stand Up Paddleboard? They're stuck out there. Some of them are swimming." We hastily assembled some washing line as a tow rope and I dispatched Mark on a SUP with a kayak paddle to effect a heroic rescue. The tide was beginning to ebb, which was starting to carry the stranded windsurfers further out to sea.

Mary hurried over "Can I ask a favour? Keith is stuck at Carnac. Could you go and get him with your van? He called from a borrowed phone, but when we rang back, the person on the other end just hung up! I'm afraid he might leave the beach if the wind gets up." We hastily exchanged phone numbers "Just ring me if he comes back." I called to Mary as I sped off to St Colomban, not feeling at all confident of finding "Un Anglais avec voile et planche – An Englishman with a board and sail" somewhere on the beach.

"You look like a man who could do with a lift!" I found Keith straight away near the windsurfing centre, sitting calmly on the wall, looking out to sea and enjoying the view. With laid-back confidence that something would turn up, all his kit was de-rigged, sails rolled and ready to go. "I brought you some water!" I said as I handed him a bottle. He was parched. We strapped his board on the roof and meandered back. It seemed that everyone had returned home successfully. Strangely, the need for a rescue always seems to happen on the night that the club members all go out for their collective meal. One previous year, a rescue of an 82-year old had been effected by a 78-year old on meal night!

Everybody looked exhausted; but their main concern was making sure they could have a shower and still get to the restaurant on time.

Eating out is not in our budget, so we didn't join them. Mary kindly gave us a bottle of red as an unnecessary but much appreciated thank you. Mark and I coiffed the wine as we chatted, watching the sky turn softly pink as the sun went down. A nearly-full moon hung like a bright bauble above the bay.

I reflected with Mark on our friend Andrew's charm offensive (and yes, that is fully intended to be an oxymoron!)

"Are those highlights in your hair or are you just grey?" he had asked me earlier, his eyes sparkling as he grinned innocently, awaiting the reaction.

He claimed not to understand what I was getting at when I answered that next time a lady asks him "Does this dress make me look fat?" the acceptable reply is "No!" – and that under no circumstances should he follow up with "It's not the dress that makes you look fat. It's your backside, stomach and thighs."

Andrew had taken me out on his quad bike earlier and admitted that with my reputation for bungee jumping, parachuting and extreme embroidery, he HAD tried to scare me.

"You coped quite well." He conceded. "For your age!"

5

"AURAY OR BUST"

An Exercise in Combative Cycling for 80-Year Olds. A Pedal with Pensioners Nearly Ends in a Fight

A 14-mile cycle ride. We set off at 10am and arrived back just before 6pm.

Eight hours, for much of which we were either lost or missing someone. We did the most technical bit of single track that I have ever ridden, which was interesting since at least half of the party were on electric shopping bikes with baskets on the handlebars. And we nearly got into a fight!

"Of course, the mistake they made was to follow Joe. He was the one who led them 40-miles around the Isle of Sheppey. He's 80-years old!" So said Keith last year when the same group had all disappeared on some lengthy marine mission of questionable directionality on their windsurfers.

Today, I had the full Joe experience all to myself – a true 'Count Arthur Strong' meets 'Last of the Summer Wine' trip. All that was missing was a bathtub sliding down a hillside with three pensioners in it. Mark was dog sitting, but had he come along, it would have been perfect. Like Compo in 'Last of the Summer Wine' who favours baler twine in lieu of a belt, Mark had embraced his own singular sense of style and had taken to holding up his shorts with a bungee cord.

"We got horribly lost last year trying to cycle back from Auray, so we'll cycle there, have lunch then get the train back." Joe shouted these instructions over his shoulder as he pedalled off, swiftly opening up a large gap between himself and the peloton. By the time we had reached Plouharnel, just up the road, we had already lost Keith. I cycled right back as far as the war museum, where I found Keith waiting patiently for Joe. "He stopped to take photos!" Keith said, but Joe had sped on his way again so fast that Keith had missed it.

The route we took to Auray bore little resemblance to the pleasant and scenic route that I remember cycling with Steve in previous years. Steve's route had meandered along the river, passed dolmens (standing stones) in fragrant country lanes and wound through oyster beds along the coastline – and had included the all-important ice-cream stop at La Trinitée sur Mer. I explained our route to Mark when I got back. "You know that huge roundabout that you come around on the main road from Vannes? We cycled round that." It was all but a motorway! It was every man for himself as we ran the gauntlet like newly-fledged ducklings left to take our chances amid the traffic. Or maybe it was more like lemmings.

We passed through a few industrial estates before we hit a dual carriageway where Joe told us "If we get separated, follow the signs to the port of St Goustin." Of course, we got separated. Somehow, the group managed to approach our lunch stop from three completely different directions – Joe and I from the direction of Vannes after taking a wrong turn, which I wouldn't have minded except that it was UP A HILL!

It was over lunch that we discovered another flaw in the planning. We had been looking at the wrong day on the train timetable. It was 12.30 and the next train that would take bikes back to the campsite at Penthièvre was not until 4pm. "We'll cycle back!" went up the rallying cry from the table; I don't know if it was bravado or just the fact that most of us had by now put away at least one boule de cidre. I was all for getting the train back, but as the most junior member of the group by a couple of decades, I felt honour bound not to wimp out.

Powered by pancakes, cidre and caffeine, we set off. In entirely the wrong direction. "We should have the sun on our right shoulder" observed Barry. His bike was not going to let us get away with it, however and raised its own directional objection in puncture form.

Puncture duly repaired, we set off back the way we had come, the sun now scorching satisfyingly on our right shoulders. I looked over mine and remarked that I could see no sign of Barry and Jan. I rode back to find them struggling with Barry's wheel, which was not on properly following the puncture repair. We fixed it, caught up the others (Joe had stopped eventually) and continued.

We turned off the road to follow a cycle track. This took us along the most technical piece of single track that I have ever ridden – a steep, narrow downhill, through trees, with protruding stones and roots and a sharp left hander at the bottom. Those of us on mountain bikes managed OK, but after struggling with the first part, the electric shopping bikes split off and said rather sensibly that they would return home via the road.

The real beauty of our cycle track, however, was that it

took us in a perfect circle and we ended up exactly where we had started. The shopping bike splinter group looked rather surprised when, after back-tracking, they had re-joined us!

"Never mind. We can go and see the 'A-lee-na-monts'" Joe said. "The what?" "The Alignments". I have to say that I never tire of seeing the thousands of amazing standing stones at Carnac. I also saw a silvery-gold Breton foal with a beautiful star in the centre of his forehead. The Breton is a very rare breed of heavy horse, but the camera took a while to wake up and Joe was off before I could take a photo of the foal.

A map check on the verge of a narrow road, near a sharp bend, in some welcome shade did nothing for Anglo-French relations. A Frenchman stopped his car behind us, switched off his engine and started gesticulating. "I think he is saying he can't get past" we decided en group. We moved even further off the road and he moved his car right up to us and switched off his engine again, continuing to gesticulate furiously. By this time Maurice was on the corner indicating that it was clear for the Frenchman's car to pass. Joe strolled over for a chat with the man in his perfect French. "I can't pass, you need to get to the side!" "We are at the side!" Joe replied.

At this point, a young lady in a Land Rover sailed past, overtaking the Frenchman and rounding the corner in a rather carefree, laissez-faire manner. Being overtaken by a girl in a large vehicle rather weakened his "I can't get past" position. "I'll go and have a word with him..." Barry said, his jaw set. Jan called him back. "If my brother was here, he'd have had him out of the car and in the bushes by now!" Undeterred, the Frenchman crawled past us, millimetres from our handlebars, just to make a point. The point being that he was a grumpy, old git, spoiling for some trouble.

Joe shot ahead once we got back to Plouharnel. "They all know the way back from here!" Once again, his words drifted back to us over his shoulder as he disappeared over the horizon like Bradley Wiggins. Our group arrived back at the campsite in dribs and drabs between 6.00 and 6.30pm, having cycled about forty miles in 27-degree heat.

Not quite the 3pm return we had planned, but then, there was no wind anyway.

However, I did have one large regret. Another huge MISS on the appropriate song lyric front. I have long bemoaned the missed opportunity to deploy 'Donald Wheer's Your Troosers?' when I took my Uncle Don a cup of tea one morning. Following my knock, he had appeared at the bedroom door wearing a string vest and a pair of long, white underpants. I was too taken aback to burst into song, which is a shame. Opportunities of such perfection are few and far between – AND we were on the Isle of Skye, which is even given a mention in the song.

This MISS was almost as bad. Not keen on the cycling aspect, Barbara had come along on the train to join us for lunch. Joe had organised a taxi to take her back to the station at Auray.

Why oh why did I not cast my mind to Vanessa Paradis, the former Mrs Johnny Depp and think to say when it arrived "Joe – le Taxi"?

6

BREAK FOR THE BORDER; 1ST STOP – RADON, NORMANDY

Boys Behaving Badly & Creepy Crevettes; & The French DO Have A Word For 'Entrepreneur'

I walked the dogs before our departure from Penthièvre and my little friend in a micro tent, who was having a wash at the drinking water tap, started on about the dogs. Last night he had asked me why on earth I had four before adding "One dog is e-nuff. What about your 'usband?!"

It seemed he was being a little tongue-in-cheek. "They are your friends?" he asked that morning. I told him that they gave me much love and joy. "We must thank the Lord for dogs!" he replied.

That was not exactly how I felt a few minutes later. The plan had been to walk the dogs in the woods rather than on the beach, so that we could make our onward journey dry, sand-free and accompanied by a baguette, for the plan had also included a trip to the bakery. Then, with impeccable timing, Rosie went missing. Luckily, as happened several times last year, she had simply gone back to the caravan, although I learned later that she was a little put out that when she got there, Mark was not around. He had the audacity to be away emptying the toilet rather than doing his duty by providing a permanent welcome committee on the off chance that she might, at any time, decide to return, unannounced.

Due to Operation Overload, our departure for Europe had been delayed, so we were making a break for the border. We had decided to cross France in just two days so that we would not be too far behind schedule when we began our trip across Germany. We got away from the campsite at 10:04, which was a miracle. We lost a little time at the bakery, making up Rosie's deficit of one baguette - and hastily adding some emergency almond croissants and a lemon cake, just in case, but we were still under way in good time.

It was a long, straight drive to Radon – not a radioactive gas which seeps up through your floorboards in Cornwall, but a pretty village in Lower Normandy. The campsite was very sweet, and Monsieur solicitously parked us well away from a large group of children.

I filled the water tank. I thought that I might as well not fill it to the top, since we were staying for only one night. Unfortunately, I misjudged it slightly and found that there wasn't even enough water in it to cover the pump. Mark took this well.

It looked like it might rain, so I pushed the windsurf boards under the caravan "We don't want things to get wet." I explained.

I got the full weight of his razor-sharp riposte; "Yes – we wouldn't want anything to get wet. Like the pump or the inside of the water tank..."

Well, that's just not big and it's not clever!

We took the pups on a picturesque evening stroll into

the village of Radon, through a wood and past a field of beautiful thoroughbred horses with their foals. We were joined by a rather boisterous Labrador who just wouldn't go home. We were really worried about him. As we got to Radon, he started to wander all over the road. I think he was well known, however. Our minds were put at rest when one of the locals had a quick word in his ear and he galloped off home!

I was missing some garlic, so while we were in the village, I stocked up on that, a creditable bottle of Cabernet Sauvignon for €3.80 and some ear spray. My ears had been blocked since we left the UK. They nearly blew off when I realised that the bottle of spray for which I paid more than €11 was simply purified sea water. Until that morning, my lugholes could have availed themselves of the whole of the Gulf de Morbihan completely free of charge!

A couple of village lads shouted and approached us on their bikes. They were carrying a small, blue fishing net which was bulging with a mud-coloured mass. "Cinq Euros, Madame!" they offered. I saw that in fact, the mud-coloured mass had claws and eyes and various other bits of exoskeleton protruding from it. "Crevettes, Madame!" they said proudly. It was not hard to decline. Heaven only knew where they had dredged them up from – or when – but I admired their enterprise.

It rather put me in mind of the other morning at the campsite in Penthièvre when Mark had taken the dogs for their morning pee poo. He heard a shout; "Let me hold your dog, LET ME HOLD YOUR DOG!" A young lad who was camping with a large group of youngsters had run up to Mark. "If you let me hold your dog, that girl over there, she'll get naked!"

"No, don't let him hold your dog. DON'T LET HIM

HOLD YOUR DOG!" but it was too late. The lead had already changed hands. Rosie is a trained therapy dog, but this was not what we had in mind. She has had a profound influence on the lives of the elderly and we are glad of that, but we hope that she has had a less profound influence on the lives of the young...

And to think that former U.S. President George W. Bush allegedly said; "The trouble with the French is; they have no word for 'Entrepreneur'!"

7

BREAK FOR THE BORDER – NE FRANCE; SÉZANNE TO VILSBERG

"Let's Off Road!"; A cute bull ('though his mum was a cow) & The Legend of the Storks

If you want to experience adrenaline; drive a large caravan around Paris.

To increase the thrill still further; be a passenger in the tow vehicle!

I still judge all Parisian driving experiences against The Arc de Triomphe. We drove into Paris many years ago, fully aware of the Arc's notoriety. We tried very hard to avoid it but found that in Paris, the gravitational pull of The Arc is inexorable.

Our unintended transit of the Arc was hindered by the fact that we didn't realise that unlike on UK roundabouts, right of way rests with those COMING INTO the Arc – not those already doing the rounds. This led to several stand-offs in quick succession. French people drove straight at us with the sort of manic determination in their eyes that said "This is for Agincourt!"

There are a lot of entrances on to the Arc. There were a

lot of stand-offs. All that was missing was the heraldry and the lances.

We experienced the same wild-eyed challenges on the périphérique with the caravan, although being a motorway, this was a much more sustained experience and the stakes were higher. We had with us our only home on wheels. On the Arc de Triomphe, we were dealing only with cars and I had rapidly resolved The Arc situation by putting the map over my face so that I couldn't see what was going on, then telling Mark to get off at any exit and we'd sort out our directions from there. On the périphérique, we had no such retreat available from the lunatic Lithuanian lorries, who headed directly at us and gave no quarter.

Once clear of Paris, we followed the A4 for miles. It was a good straight road, but the surface was so bumpy that the retractable jockey wheel at the front of the caravan actually came loose, fell down and started dragging along the road.

We stopped at Sézanne, a beautiful, medieval city. The Municipal Campsite there was our cheapest ever at €8 Euros per night. There were lovely walks straight from site into the woods where, if I understood the signage correctly, Limoniers grew lemons to improve the soil for nearby Champagne. Thank you, Limoniers!

A bunch of Rufty Tufty Belgian off-roaders turned up in their Land Rovers and made our evening by lighting a fire with sticks. We watched intently, earnestly hoping to see them cook up some road kill. The men all started off bare chested and in shorts. Even when they were just standing around, they all struck poses, as though they were being filmed, which in fact they were. By me, pretending to take photos of Kai. Dad was so muscle-bound that he could barely get his arms down by his sides. Mum was wearing cargo pants to look the part, but just seemed a bit uncomfortable with it all. I loved that they had tents that popped up on the roofs of their Land Rovers. Great for keeping at bay all the wild animals, poisonous snakes and deadly insects that you find when you're on safari in the campsites of rural France.

I'm afraid that for us, any sense of off-roading as a cool pursuit has been utterly ruined by the incompetent off-roaders Simon and Lindsey on 'The Fast Show'; "It's gripped. It's sorted. LET'S OFF ROAD!" Mark and I sniggered while exchanging cool 'shaka' hand gestures with each other.

...

The following morning, I was really wishing that those Belgians would hurry up. We needed to get packed up and go but we couldn't stop watching them. I suppose it was no surprise that they were so entertaining. They were, after all, from the country that gave us Tin Tin, Plastic Bertrand and Jean Claude Van Damme.

Then, the punchline. On our way out through Sézanne, we saw the Belgian off-roaders verifying 'The Fast Show's' stereotype. They were stuck trying to get their Land Rover either in or out of a parking space that I would have rated Mark's chances of navigating with the caravan in tow. "LET'S OFF ROAD!"

Mark had been so engrossed with the Belgians that he drove the van over the Road Refresher dog bowl again. It recovered from being completely flat with only one small crack in the rim. We seem to be repeating a few of last year's disasters. We hoped that our axle was still bearing up – especially after our rumpety-bumpety trip along the A4.

...

Three omens seemed to be warning us against going to our destination; Germany. Torrential rain; Riots in Hamburg - and every campsite that we had checked had a one-dog policy.

We had already re-routed ourselves north of our original itinerary through Bavaria. This was because the weather forecast for Beautiful Bayern and the Black Forest predicted rain every single day for the whole of July!

We saw our first field of sunflowers – and a stork. Perhaps this was where the margarine companies originally came for both raw material and branding inspiration for their product.

Our campsite in Vilsberg was quirky but picturesque, located in what seemed to be a disused quarry. The owners could not have been lovelier and there was so much to do in the area – the beautiful villages of Alsace and her famous wine trail, the Maginot line and a boat lift, to name but a few.

I have fond memories of Alsace. I have visited a number of times and it was the exotic destination for my first ever trip abroad on a school exchange visit to learn French. I think that the children from this paradise who visited the northern, industrial town of Blackburn, Lancashire, got the thin end of the exchange wedge!

Once we had got Kismet's legs down and pitched, we did a lovely walk around Vilsberg but we had to cut it short as Kai seemed to be suffering. It was very warm, and he kept asking to be carried. Mark panicked as I led us fearlessly through a field containing some sweet-looking cattle. "Jackie – that's a BULL! Stop taking photographs..." Mark was even less amused when I quipped "The bull's OK, but his Mum was a cow."

The bull was pretty laid back but there did seem to be a high incidence of quite ferocious, tethered guard / farm dogs straining on their chains or snarling behind high fences as we strolled through Vilsberg.

Our closest neighbour on the campsite was a lovely Dutch family. The parents were both teachers. They told us that they were away for six weeks, but the Dad said that he had some exam papers to mark. We asked him what subject. "Comparative Administration." He replied. Wow. 6,000 words apiece. I'll bet he was looking forward to that! Luckily, he had only twelve of them.

So, we had successfully made our break for the border. Tomorrow, we would enter Germany.

...

The Legend of the Storks

Throughout Alsace in the spring, storks can be seen on huge nests that they build on the chimney pots of houses. The folklore of the storks in Alsace goes back a long way. It is linked to Louis the Pious, son of Charlemagne, who, in 817 decided to split his lands between his three sons.

Louis might have been Pious, but he was definitely a bit flaky when it came to integrity. His second wife persuaded him to go back on his promise to his other sons and make his son with her his heir. The three other sons rebelled and waged war against their father.

The storks were upset by the bloodshed and asked God to end it. However, God said that He had given Man free will, so He would not intervene. God's like that. God gave the storks permission to dip their wings in black as mourning for the chaos that descended on their homeland - and that is why the symbolic storks of Alsace have black tips on their wings.

Unlike Louis, storks are very faithful and loyal. They usually return to the same nest and partner each year. Nesting storks bring good luck to the house and local legend states that storks will not nest on a house where there has been a divorce.

When a baby is born, it is because a stork flew to the underground lake where the souls of the dead are reincarnated as babies, wrapped one in a sheet and delivered it to the new parents.

I'll bet that you didn't know that the legend of babies being brought by storks originated in Alsace!

8

VILSBERG TO HEIDELBERG – TALES OF THE UNEXPECTED IN GERMANY

We cross The Rhine into a land of traffic jams, disregard for H&S & flexibility with rules

We thought we were going to take a souvenir of Vilsberg with us. We had to drive through a Monument Historique – an arch quoted as 2.8m high. We are 2.6m high... It was a close one. Thankfully, our trust in the Sat Nav was not misplaced.

And driving through the Vosges National Park was a pleasant start to a Friday.

The terrain had certainly changed as we entered Alsace, an area which has been both German and French many times over the centuries. We were certainly in Gerani-land, passing rows of pretty Hansel and Gretel houses. The towns were no longer 'Villes' but had become Heims, Dorfs and Willers, even though we had not yet crossed the border.

I always hated geraniums and hydrangeas, but I now seem to have come to terms with them. I don't know if it is an age thing – a sudden enlightened appreciation for gaudy flowers. Somehow in France, they just look right.

Hydrangeas add a lovely splash of cobalt or puce to the outside of the grey, stone Breton cottages and geraniums just look happy; tumbling from the balconies of Alpine chalets and brightening up the window boxes of Germanic, timber-framed houses.

We had a bit of a pfaff in Pfaffenheim. The Sat Nav had a 'moment' and we turned into a housing estate. A man was shaking his head vigorously to express certainty on a point that we had already grasped; that we had gone the wrong way with our 7.35m caravan. He asked us where we were going.

"Germany."

"This is not the way to Germany!"

He didn't look overly convinced that the rather minis-cule main road that we were on was the way to Germany either, but we were taking the scenic route (and avoiding tolls!)

Then we crossed the Rhine. It immediately started rain-ing. Within fifteen minutes, we hit a traffic jam and were cut up by a Porsche. Welcome to Germany. We felt utterly miserable and stressed.

"There's a town in Germany called Wank." I told Mark.

"It should all be called that!" he replied.

Today had been our shortest journey so far; just over 100 miles, but it had taken the longest.

"If we overtake someone from Holland, does that mean we Pass the Dutchy on the Left-Hand Side?" I quipped. He gave me one of those looks.

"No." He said. "Holland is not a Duchy, so it would need to be a Luxembourger."

It was still raining. And we were still in a traffic jam. However, as you can see, we never fail to cheer each other up.

We both uttered a proper "I don't BELIEVE it!" when we saw a lorry carrying Category 8 Corrosives without the correct safety plates.

It turned out that this was by no means the last thing that would be unexpected in Germany.

...

Well, at least something had to go our way. I attempted to check in to our first choice of campsite near Heidelberg. Like all of the others, it advertised a 1-dog policy.

"How many persons?"

"Two".

"Any Dogs?"

"We have four dogs. They are very small and well behav..."

"A hot shower costs €1 for four minutes. We can order bread in the morning. Choose any spot."

I didn't even need to justify Die Hunde by saying that they were well behaved!

We chose our spot overlooking the River Neckar. We had some interesting neighbours – some very run-down cara-vans that looked like they were permanently occupied. They resembled the tumbledown beach house in the film 'Local Hero'. Such a blatant show of poverty was a little unex-pected in Europe's most advanced economic powerhouse.

It would have been a tranquil spot were it not for the road and railway on the opposite bank of the river, with a hillside behind acting like a sound baffle to direct the sound straight at us. We were entertained into the night by party riverboats coming past, adding drunken renditions of YMCA to the soundscape. We hoped that they were doing all the actions. Still, after driving 692 miles in the last three days, we fully intended to do a Frankie Goes to Hollywood and – RELAX!

...

I felt like a tourist, unable to speak a word of German. 'German in Three Months' had remained stubbornly closed since we bought it, probably about three months ago. I was embarrassed at having to ask the chap on reception "Do you speak English?" straight away as I checked in. I did tell him "Je parle Français, e parlo Italiano" by which I meant, "I am not just one of those British tourists who goes around Europe talking loudly and expecting everyone to speak my language."

"That's no good in Germany." He observed, perfectly correctly.

The family in the camper van next door also asked if I spoke German when I kept having to retrieve Lani. I felt even more embarrassed, so 'German in Three Months' came out. I did a chapter on 'The' and while it is not as complex as the twelve words that the Italian language boasts for the definite article, I still had to have a lie down afterwards.

So, I tried the Winston Churchill method; learning five words a day. This proved difficult, as I couldn't remember five German words in one go, so I opted for a SMART target (Simple, Memorable, Achievable, Realistic, Timely.) The 'Achievable' part meant just one word each day.

I started with "Entschuldigung" or "excuse me." I couldn't remember that either. I tried the ruse that I had used to cram for many an exam; read what you need to remember last thing at night and then sleep on it. It worked a treat – as a brain washing tactic. The next morning, I couldn't even remember which word I had learnt, never mind what the German for it was.

It took three days just to master 'Entschuldigung'. Not quite as timely as I had in mind, but it soon came in useful. "Entschuldigung, Deutsche nicht sprecken." Well, apologising in German for not speaking German shows at least a little more effort and forethought than launching straight in with an introductory "Do you speak English?"

9

DON'T TRY TO PARK A VAN
IN HEIDELBERG

Max Planck and Scotty from Star Trek disagree on "Ye cannae change the laws of Physics." However, Physics Still Dictates that "Ye Cannae Park A Van in Heidelberg!"

Heidelberg. At last. I thought I had applied for a job here when I left University many years ago. Everyone told me how beautiful Heidelberg was and how much I would enjoy it. It turned out the job was in Hamburg, which is considerably less charming. Thankfully, I didn't get it anyway!

We drove in along the river Neckar. Although all public transport was dog-friendly, we thought that it would be easier to drive into town...

We drove around for an hour or so, looking for a parking space. On the up side, it was very pretty. "There is a big 'P' marked on the map at the bus station, we could try that." I suggested.

Mark declined and programmed every Parking Platz into the Sat Nav in order. All the surface, roadside parking was full and all of the car parks were underground – and you can't get a 1.89m high van under a 1.8m car park barrier, even when you have taken all the SUPs off the roof for that very reason. We eventually found a parking space where the big 'P' was marked on the map at the bus station. I let it pass.

Well, almost.

Like Basil Fawlty and The War, I might have mentioned it once. But I think I got away with it.

We paid €9 for three hours parking to a bloke in a high-vis jacket on a bicycle. "Do you think he's official?" I asked Mark. I only asked because I once paid a couple of quid to a bloke in an authoritative-looking peaked hat who was helping people to park in Temple Bar in the centre of Dublin. I was told later that he was anything but official – he just appeared every night, charged people a small fee to help them to park and then, when he had collected enough money, he disappeared and blew the lot on Guinness!

We wandered around the Altstade. That means 'Old Town' – not high town, which would have been more like it after all the hills we walked up. There is a funicular if you want to save your legs.

The view was worth it, though. The Altstade is a beautiful citadel next to a river with a large sandstone castle keep. A bit like Carlisle.

Schloss Heidelberg dominates the city. The castle really does span the centuries. Some of it was built in 1933! Some of it was struck by lightning and some of it was pinched for building the rest of Heidelberg.

Mark mocked me for taking a photo of the pups next to a picture of the Universe with Heidelberg pinpointed at its centre, but it was my 'Homage' to Max Planck, who has four Institutes in Heidelberg. Max Planck invented Quantum Leap, that famous 1980s Sci Fi series – and won the Nobel Prize for it.

Max Planck disagrees fundamentally with Scotty on Star

Trek, who is famous for his hypothesis that "Ye cannae change the Laws of Physics." Max Planck reckons "We have no right to assume that any physical laws exist, or if they have existed up until now, that they will continue to exist in a similar manner in the future."

Blimey. It is no wonder that no-one understands Quantum Theory. Not even the Lovely, Lovely Professor Brian Cox. Not even National Treasure Stephen brain-the-size-of-the-universe Fry.

Anyway, after all that cogitation we decided "Es ist Bier o Uhr – It is Beer O'clock". We treated ourselves to two Weiß-bier – wheat beers (a light and a dark one) for €3.90 each plus €3.50 each for a panino right in the centre of Heidelberg. Reasonable prices. That was certainly not something that we had expected in Germany.

Die Hunde went down a storm. At the castle, where it cost us €3.50 for a small bottle of water and 50 cents each to pee, we were told; "We don't do tap water. Oh. For the dogs? Of course!"

We also had some cake balls; Heidelberger Kurfurstenkugel made from an original 1896 recipe. They were so weighty and substantial that they would not have been out of place had they been fired out of a cannon. Mind, after all that sightseeing, we were in need of some hearty sustenance.

10

HEIDELBERG TO UFFENHEIM – FERRY ACROSS THE NECKAR!

Caravan Kismet goes Rafting

A bill for €93 for three nights. Now that WAS what we expected in Germany. Our most expensive campsite EVER - and they still had the brass face to levy extra for using the shower. There was a charge for the pitch, for each person, for the tow vehicle, €10 per night for four dogs, for electricity (Strom) and for something else that we didn't quite manage to translate but was probably Tourist Tax.

We drove up the River Neckar through Dilsberg, which was just as beautiful as Heidelberg. We saw a lot of it, as it too had that seemingly unavoidable German feature – a traffic jam. It gave us plenty of time to peruse the sights. Unfortunately, the bridge that we needed to cross the Neckar was closed, but since there was another long traffic jam back the way we came, we decided to push on regardless.

How bad could it be?

We followed the river for miles and miles with absolutely no sign of another bridge. Our confidence was wavering as bends in the road seemed to be taking us away from our destination. Then the Sat Nav took us down a narrow little lane to the Neckar before confidently instructing us to 'Take the Ferry.'

We looked around for a while before we spotted something on the opposite bank - a few planks of wood strapped together with an engine stuck to one end. The last time I saw a craft like that, I had constructed it myself on an Outdoor Activity Course.

It sank.

"If it doesn't cost a fortune, it will be a laugh!" said Mark. "If it's about a tenner, let's do it, but if it's, like, £30 we'll not bother." I walked down to ask the ferryman whether he thought it would be feasible to get Big Blue and Kismet's 12m length aboard without sinking his ferry. I still couldn't remember my word for 'excuse me – Entschuldigung' – but luckily our man spoke English and seemed pretty sanguine about the idea of transporting us.

I suddenly remembered a priceless piece of travel advice from songster Chris de Burgh; "Don't pay the Ferryman" he urged. Mr de Burgh went further and suggested that a price should not even be fixed until the crossing had been completed. Still, when the ferryman proffered a fare of €3.80 then knocked it down to €3.40, I had to ask. "3.40 Euros? Not €340?" I was incredulous. I think even Cautious Chris de Burgh might have coughed up less than the cost of a panino in the centre of Heidelberg in advance.

I waved Mark down towards the boarding ramp. We grounded out our jockey wheel as we embarked and Kismet's backside was hanging over the end for the fish to look at, but the ferry, like our spirits, remained buoyant. "This is what independent travel is all about. A bit of adventure..." we gloated. We had to ask the ferryman where we were, as we had absolutely no idea.

The back of the caravan hit the deck getting up the steep incline as we disembarked. A small child chased us up the road brandishing a few bits of Kismet that had parted company on the dismount. Besides €3.40, it cost us the foot off a corner steady and a bit of a scrape to the undercarriage, but it helped us get en route in the right direction. We had been travelling for an hour and a half, but were still only twelve miles closer to our destination!

This wasn't the end of our adventure, however. We went through some tiny villages and in Neckarberg, I had to get out and direct traffic. The single street through the village was so narrow that only one vehicle could pass through. Big Blue had to drive virtually into someone's garden and kiss their front door in order to let a bus go by in the opposite direction. Needless to say, the ever-patient cars behind got right up close and personal, so we couldn't then reverse. I had to direct them past in order, starting from the back of the queue. "Entschuldigung. Entschuldigung."

We pitched up in Uffenheim after a stop for diesel at €1.08 (bargain!) and a trip to Netto. (German food prices surprised us too – they were very similar to the UK and unlike in Italy, you could buy mangoes.) Mark dispatched me with a shopping list for all the essentials; "Get biscuits, chocolate and Weißbier!" he commanded.

We had rather a lot of laundry to do, so we settled for a day of jobs and sitting in the sun. Our neighbours were very friendly. A chap and his wife in a camper van chatted away with us – they really loved Die Hunde. A German lady who spoke no English but had a little dog came over and demanded that our English-speaking neighbour translate to tell us about a really nice off-lead dog walk locally.

As we sat in the sun, we listened to the kids playing in the swimming pool next door. We had free access to the pool from the campsite if we collected a ticket from reception. The children all played so harmoniously, it was actually pleasant to listen to. I am sure that in England there would have been some Horrible Horace who would have jumped on someone's head and tried to drown them.

Every now and again we heard an announcement over the loudhailer in German. I realised that unfortunately, the only time that I had really heard German spoken, especially on a loudhailer, was on war films.

11

A FAIRY-TALE OF ROTHENBURG OB DER TAUBER

A Real GOB – Get Onyer Bucketlist!

Fairy-tale city I was promised. Fairy-tale city I got. Rothenburg ob der Tauber is truthfully THE most beautiful place that I have ever visited.

Who needs Disneyland when real places like that exist?

Since entering Germany, we had been unable to escape the Laws of Physics. According to 'The Hitchhiker's Guide to the Galaxy' the Answer to Life, The Universe and Everything is 42 - and that is the number of towers on the medieval walls of Rothenburg ob der Tauber. We walked the walls and were treated to far-reaching views across the Tauber valley. It was 27°C at 9am in the morning, but thankfully, the covered, wooden walkway and the gardens beneath were beautifully shady. As we passed the Dominican Convent by the corner tower of the main Burgtor Gate, strains of the Ave Maria played on a violin drifted around us. It could not have been more idyllic.

A passer-by took our photo with an 8ft high wooden toy soldier. "So that is it." Mark said. "We have clearly reached the Kingdom of 'Far Far Away'!" It was true and, as in Shrek, we had travelled there with a donkey. (Albeit our donkey was in sausage form and had been purchased in secret from the horse butcher on the market in Brittany...)

If, like Roy Wood and Wizzard, you 'Wish it could be Christmas Every Day' then Rothenburg ob der Tauber is for you. The oversized toy soldier guards the entrance to the largest Christmas Village in Europe – and it is open all year round. So, if sweltering summer temperatures get you all in the mood for bauble buying and pressie purchasing, get down there RIGHT NOW in yer Santa shorts!

The dogs went down as storm again – mainly with American tourists. "Ain't they CUTE?! I LOVE their liddle curlicues!" – whatever those might be.

...

Rothenburg Recommendations

Philip rocked up to our campsite in an enormous motorhome. "I live just up the road but when it gets over 30°C I come out in my RV because it has aircon!" he told us. We met because the dogs shot out and scared his little girl, Mara. We apologised profusely, and his wife was lovely about it. Far from getting the telling off that you would expect from an English parent, bristling with intolerance and entitlement, she brought Mara over to meet the dogs – and then Philip gave us loads of recommendations of places to visit. We thanked them again, not only for the recommendations, but for just being so cool!

- Dinkelsbuhl – a beautiful city which, like Rothenburg ob der Tauber, is on Germany's 'Romantic Road'

- Sommerhausen – a medieval, walled town from which you can walk to the magnificent city of Wùrtzburg
- Fränkische Seenplatte – Waldcamping in Pleinfeld is the nicer one (in woods) while Seecamping in Langlau is next to the lake for windsurfing
- Altmühlsee – good for windsurfing
- Vilsalpsee – a good lake for SUP
- Tannheimer Tal – voted 3rd best for hiking!
- Ulsenheim – Winery Meier is the best

There is always more to see and never enough time. I am not keen on retracing my steps, but I would definitely visit Rothenberg ob der Tauber again. Even without all of these other wonders, Rothenberg ob der Tauber is a definite a GOB – Get Onyer Bucketlist!

12

DOG ON THE RHINE – EIN SCHEISSTAG, CAMPSITE SONNENSTRAND, BACHARACH

A Bad Day Which Started Badly, Went Badly - & Then Got Worse...

It started with spilt milk. No point crying over that but I did cry when we nearly died while joining the Autobahn.

It was something that we had never encountered before – a 'Give Way' (unmarked and unsigned) instead of a slip road on to the motorway. All I remember is the back of a 40-tonne tautliner swinging across our nose and any semblance of the lane in front of us (the one that we had thought was a slip road) disappearing with horrific speed.

In shock and feeling desolate, I snivelled as we drove past more traffic jams in the rain. Things didn't improve after we had set up at our campsite; Sonnenstrand in Bacharach. Lani suddenly became really poorly and we both honestly thought we were going to lose her. I had been playing ball with her when she suddenly vomited so violently that she cried out in pain and ran whimpering into my arms. She was very, very sick, vomiting white foam, her tongue and gums went very pale and she became so wobbly that she was unable to stand up.

I pleaded with Mark to go and get details of a vet from reception as I was concerned that she had been poisoned. The dogs had all been playing in the Rhine and there was some weed along the bank. Never one to overreact, I had managed to convince myself that it was toxic blue-green algae. As we both expected, since it was out-of-hours, there was no answer from the vet. It was either going to be that or an answer in German that we didn't understand. I just needed to feel that we were DOING something.

We rang the emergency number of our own vet. They reassured us and told us just to keep an eye on Lani. I hadn't seen her drink excessively, but she had been playing in the river and after a hot car journey, had possibly drunk or accidentally ingested lots of water. She does enjoy pawing the water and then snapping at the bubbles that she creates.

Our English neighbours, Mary and Andy were very sweet and concerned. Lani settled with me and slept, curled up in the curve of my tummy. Our poor little girl was so weak. We set up the sofa bed in the caravan and Mark slept there with Lani, so that she could have a settled night's sleep without being disturbed by the other dogs.

All in all, it was a bit of ein Scheißtag – a sh** day!

...

The best sound that we had heard for some time was Rosie grumbling at Lani the following morning. The annoying little sister had started doing her thing; swinging off Rosie's beard and licking Rosie's face in the manner of someone using their tongue to creosote a fence. It looked like our little Pocket Rocket was back on form and I can't tell you how happy that made us. She polished off a bland, invalid's breakfast of white fish and rice like she hadn't eaten for weeks. We couldn't believe that she had recovered so quickly from being so unbelievably sick.

Nevertheless, we decided to take it easy with Lani. We had a very lazy morning; we got up late then went back to bed for a snooze for about three hours. It was a lovely warm day, so we got out the SUPs and paddled out to the island in the middle of the Rhine. Mark, of course, had to go and try to shoot some rapids. He fell off and was able to boast a nice bruise to the hip.

I really wished that I had taken my camera to get a shot of Pups on SUPs with the impressive fortress of Burg Stahlek on the hillside behind, although with the way our luck was running, I would have probably dropped it in the river.

Bacharach was a lovely spot. The campsite was triangular in shape and we had the thin end of the wedge. We were parked right next to the water at the narrow, quieter end of the campsite. Little silver fish were jumping in the shallows and we had a beautiful view across the river to a church spire and the vineyards on the hillsides opposite. We even had a loo with a view. The bathroom window afforded a magnificent view of Burg Stahleck.

We planned to stay for a while.

13

DOG ON THE RHINE – A QUICK WAY TO GET SCHLOSSED!

Wine Walks, Wine Tastings & A Rundtour

A word of advice. If you don't like castles, wine and half-timbered houses, do not come to the Rhineland.

It was another hot, sunny day, so we waited until it cooled a little to take the dogs out for a walk. We ambled into Bacharach, a pretty cobbled town with lovely old, timber-framed houses. Following a pathway up to the vine-yards, we were treated to beautiful views across the rooftops of the town.

We had forgotten to take any water with us and the doggies were hot, so we cut our walk short, but vowed to come back the following day. We dropped back to one of the wineries and sat on a table shaded by vines. There was nothing for it. We ordered a dog bowl and a wine tasting!

My knowledge of German wines revolves largely around the generic 'Hock' as well the branded 'Black Tower', 'Blue Nun' and 'Liebfraumilch'. These were pretty much the only wines with which we were able to assault our palates in the 1980s. Wine was relatively expensive in those days – and these served with cheese or one of Delia's exotic dishes, such as Spaghetti Bolognese, were deemed to be the height of sophistication. My personal favourite was Black Tower, because as a student, the oddly-shaped and textured bottle could be re-purposed into a nice candle-holder to cement your savoir faire amid your peers. I like to refer to this decorative re-purposing of alcohol containers as 'piss artistry', although a Black Tower candle always remained a poor second to the much coveted (but in my case never achieved) Mateus Rosé lamp.

Mark and I chose a selection of six glasses of dry, local wines. We started with a light Rivaner, 'an everyday wine', which we found thin and a bit flabby. Then a 'typical Reisling', which was OK but a bit flowery. The Kerner was slightly unpleasant although the 'tender Sylvaner from the foot of Stahlek Castle' was my favourite. Then we had Blanc de Noir – a white wine made from red grapes followed by a red wine, Spatburgunder, which tasted exactly like blackcurrant cordial.

A couple of Kiwi wine connoisseurs-cum-Kiwifruit farmers joined us, which was fun. They were a little more knowledgeable (and possibly pretentious) than us about wines. For example, they knew nothing of the Mateus Rosé lamp. However, we did all agree that these examples did nothing to change our decades-old view of German wines.

...

On a cloudy, sunny day, we decided to walk up to Burg Stahlek, the castle that overlooks Bacharach. We ascended the steep steps from the town centre and stopped in the castle courtyard to take in the panoramic views over the Rhine, while enjoying an ice lolly. Burg Stahlek means 'impregnable castle' – although these days, the castle is a rather spectacular Youth Hostel.

We had thought to walk back across the valley and continue from where we had been yesterday, but instead we started following red signs which indicated 'the Rundtour'. It led us on wide, shady tracks through a forest to the village of Steeg.

There we met a chap with a small pug called Ludwig. The chap didn't seem to get that we didn't understand German and chatted away with us. We understood some of what he said; he was giving us directions, but we managed to convey that he was sending us back the way we had come. We continued upwards, following signs to Burg Stahlberg. We had mixed up Burg Stahlberg and Burg Stahlek and kept wondering why the signs said that the castle was so close, yet we were about 7km from Bacharach.

We wound up out of Steeg through more forest, with spectacular slate caverns hidden in the rock. We were treated to an awesome view across the valley of the ruins of Berg Stahlberg. "We will have to come back and visit that!" we vowed.

We continued our walk – the direction finding was very easy with signs at every crossroad as well as along the way to confirm your choice. We were delighted that our route did eventually happen upon the ruins of Burg Stahlberg, to which we had vowed to return. We sat for ages, resting in the shade while drinking in the views, the atmosphere and the history.

The return walk was across open fields, bringing us out in the vineyards above Bacharach and the Rhine. The sun had come out and the views were truly lovely. A castle to the left of me, a chateau to the right...

We were tired when we got back. We had walked 13.2km

and when we looked up details of the walk, it recommended 'strong boots.' Of course, we had done it in our sandals...

My Dad would be proud. On holiday, he once 'popped out for a little walk' and found himself on the top of Tiede, the 12,000ft volcano on Tenerife, in his sandals.

14

DOG ON THE RHINE – OOOOOOH-NING!

"It'll be back up in half an hour!"

02:14 it started raining. I got up and closed the roof lights.

06:49 we were awoken by a loud crash. I got a sense of a large person vaulting over me in bed, emitting a long and ghostly moan "Ooooooh-ning..."

We were trapped! A huge bladder of rainwater prevented us from even opening the caravan door to survey the damage. The awning was groaning and had partially collapsed. As a rainwater deflection system, the awning had failed utterly. However, had we wanted to revive the story of Noah, the roof of our awning was primed and ready to go. All it needed was a single push to unleash a tidal wave of biblical proportions. Unfortunately, the aftermath had left more than one of Mark's poles bent...

11:34 we had succumbed to a bit of a lie in. Coffee and breakfast in bed. Well, who wants to be rushing at problems on a wet Monday morning? Our neighbour, Andy, came over to help. I overheard Mark utter the immortal words from amid the wreckage "It's not as bad as it looks. It'll be back up in half an hour…"

Remarkably, as good as his word, he had the thing back up in twenty minutes and had incorporated some spectacular 'paddle vaulting'. These were additional roof supports fashioned from SUP paddles and a couple of the broken poles with their ends sheathed in protective plastic milk bottles foraged from the recycling, to prevent any sharp ends from puncturing the fabric.

It rained and rained and rained; the sort of deluge that you could only reproduce by pitching inside a car wash during a particularly heavy monsoon. Water actually started to come up through the groundsheet of the awning. Our shoes began to float around freely.

Mary and Andy had visited the night before and had rather altered our notions about German wine. They had brought in a €7 bottle of local red, Dornfelder, from Bingen, just upriver, which they had purchased from the campsite reception. It was beautiful. We immediately went to buy more.

…

You have heard about Fog on the Tyne – well here I shall tell you about Rain on the Rhine. Since it was still absolutely bucketing down, we opted for a slow start, followed by watching a film all cosied up on the bed. We had to turn the volume up to full to hear the TV over the rain hammering on our tin roof. We had been off grid to save money, but decided to get electricity to facilitate our veg with the telly all day. Solar power was definitely off the agenda.

Mark had noticed that the garage near the Lidl in Oberwesel sold LPG. An inaugural European gas bottle recharge seemed the perfect way to add excitement to a wet day. The weight of opinion had suggested that filling up our new Safefill refillable gas bottle on the Continent would be 'tricky' - in the sense that garage owners would be reluctant to allow it. We had a full set of European adaptors. We quickly worked out which adaptor was the right shape (using the same powers of deduction as a child selecting the correct piece of plastic to push through square, circular and triangular holes.) It took the garage attendant and the bloke in the van behind to help us press all the right buttons in the right order on the pump. However, finally - we got gas!

The weather was too miserable to do much other than go for a drive. We hadn't walked the day before, but I think the puppies had been glad of the rest after our long trek around the Rundtour. However, a day of rest meant that they were now fully recharged. We found a 5km circular Nordic Walking trail on metalled forest tracks and decided to brave it. Unfortunately, we got lost. It was just the perfect weather to get lost! We must have missed a turning and ended up back on the main road.

We had a few doubts about directions as we sloshed along the verge with sleek and powerful German cars whizzing past a little too closely for comfort. However, we figured that it must lead back to the parking spot, since it was signposted back to Sankt Goar, which we seemed to recall passing on the way.

I was beginning to lose all hope of ever being re-united with Big Blue when we eventually saw the sign for the parking. The sense of joy on seeing the sign was nothing to compare to the rejoicing that accompanied getting visual with a van that had not been stolen or washed away by floods – and we hadn't even lost the keys!

...

We were grateful that the view improved for our fine Rhine finale. Instead of torrential rain, we had sunshine beating down on the caravan.

After another leisurely start, we decided to walk part of the 195km Rhein Burgen Weg – The Rhine Castle Way. We did 10.2km from Burg Stahlek to Burgruine Fürstenberg. We were glad that we deigned to wear our boots after the rain. My sandals were soaked anyway, but the paths were a narrower and more challenging than those on the Rund-tour, which we had navigated in sandals.

However, just as we set off, it started to rain! We needed to print and sign a document to post back to the UK. The lovely ladies in the Tourist Office in Bacharach printed it out for us to sign, then scanned it for us to email. By the time that the ladies had finished fussing and playing with the dogs, the shower had abated.

We were treated to some fabulous views back over the Rhine and down to Bacharach. We walked past hillside villages of Neurath and Medenscheid then back via the ruins of Fürstenberg, the golden castle whose round turrets shine out on the hillside as you drive towards Bacharach. We returned to the campsite along the banks of the Rhine.

We saw a sign at Fürstenberg that said that said "use path at own risk, not suitable for people afrait of heights. Person using this path must be sure tooted." We certainly needed to be 'sure tooted' on the path that we took – it was the quick way down through a vineyard. It was extremely steep and slippery.

There were oodles of footpaths in the area and every-thing was wonderfully well signposted. We passed boards which boasted of a walk around the town walls of

Bacharach and a garden tour in Medenscheid, then there was Euro Velo 15, the long-distance cycle way that follows the Rhine from its source in Andermatt, Switzerland to the North Sea Coast at Rotterdam. However, we had spent quite a while by the Rhine in Bacharach. It was time to move on to the next part of our German adventure; Edersee. The third largest reservoir in Germany was where we were planning to avail ourselves of some windsurfing.

Instead, we got a dam big surprise!

15

"FRANKLY MY DEAR, I DO GIVE A…" – EDERSEE NATIONAL PARK

A DAM BIG SURPRISE

We turned right at Koblenz.

We had driven up the Rhine from Bacharach, carefully avoiding taking a ferry. It seemed a bit too professional for us in any case. This was a ferry that looked like boat, rather than the motorised beaver dam that had transported both us and our precious caravan over the River Neckar near Heidelberg a week or so ago.

The Dortmund leg was altogether a bit boring and industrial, although removing two ticks from Rosie and one from Mark en route helped to pass the time.

We got to our planned campsite at Binghauser, which Mark assured me was the best place for windsurfing. Mark also confirmed to me that the campsite had good reviews, although it looked crowded, wet, buggy and uninviting. The lake was extremely low, so there was a long walk through mud flats to get to the water. The campsite overlooked the mud flats and had all the appeal of a disused quarry.

"Do you speak English?" I asked the proprietor. He heaved a sigh. "Drei nacht? – Three nights?" I asked, trying to ameliorate with my limited German vocabulary. He walked out with me and spouted something in full Führer mode, with his arms going like windmills. Despite my blossoming relationship with 'German in Three Months' I didn't understand a word. "Terrasse. Left side" he barked in conclusion, indicating where he wanted us to pitch with a hand gesture that was a bit too close to a Hitler salute for my liking. Then he stalked off.

So we left.

We went back to a pretty campsite that we had seen as we passed through Affoldern. The man there didn't speak much English but shook our hands warmly as we arrived. "Anywhere here!" he showed us to a large grassy area. "See my wife at 8 o'clock tomorrow."

It rained overnight. We were beginning to get a bit fed up of German weather.

...

However, when we woke up, it was sunny, blowing a Force 5 and we were in a great windsurfing spot. There was only one thing for it.

Laundry!

We had not quite reached the same stage of desperation that had caused Mark to emulate David Beckham by wearing my sarong because he had run out of pants. Still, our clothing situation was near-critical.

The lady at the campsite was lovely and spoke perfect English. She came to settle us in, even though it was her day off. She was running a dog training session in the adjacent field. Needless to say, the campsite was very dog-friendly and we were not charged for the pups - and there was also no charge for the showers.

Our research had highlighted Edersee as a National Park and UNESCO World Heritage site – and we had come for the windsurfing. Usually, our research is very thorough, but I only realised that we were on the Eder dam, one of the targets in Guy Gibson's Operation Chastise – better known as The Dambusters – when the lady in the Tourist Office mentioned the war.

Convinced that I must be obsessed with it, she took great pains to show me "the bombardment" in the little information booklet that I bought about the local area. Maybe that was why Mr Campsite at Binghauser had been so rude to us. Around 68 local lives were lost in the floods that followed the bombing. The dam was breached during the night and the telephone reports did not reach the localities downriver in time for them to be evacuated. The flood waters had raged down the valley as far as Kassel, 35km downstream. Walking The Fab Four into the village, I had found a house with a line drawn high on the wall, which showed the level of the flood waters on the morning of 17th May, 1943.

Had we been there on that date, the contents of our entire campsite would have been washed away by a huge tidal wave.

As regards windsurfing – the Tourist Office told me that the lake was too low. In any case, the part that we were on could not be used for watersports as it was a levelling lake for the hydroelectric scheme, so it was too dangerous for recreation.

Laundry, it seemed, was definitely the best option.

...

It was sunny as I walked to the bakery. It was shut from 07:00 – 10:30, so I managed to buy two croissants and two cookies at the petrol station. Of course, being Saturday and being Germany, all the supermarkets were closed in the afternoon.

We were disappointed that we hadn't walked when we realised that there was a footpath leading up to the Eder Dam from Affoldern, a distance of only about 4km. However, we drove there and walked across the dam. We discussed whether it would have been tasteless to turn up in Lancaster Bomber costumes with 'We Woz 'Ere' emblazoned on the side. We reasoned that it was no more tasteless than the waft of burgers and waffles from the tourist industry that had grown up around the scene of what was really a terrible disaster for both sides.

We ambled along a forest path on the other side of the valley and were treated to magnificent views back across the dam and reservoir.

Looking from the top of the dam really made me wonder about the approach of large and cumbersome aeroplanes like the Lancasters of 617 Squadron, which had flown in over Waldeck Castle in the dark. I know that they had to fly very low - at 60 feet - for the bouncing bomb to work but the lake is surrounded by mountains and has several bends in it. After flying over the castle on top of its hill, the pilots had four seconds to descend into position, release the bomb and pull up the heavy plane to avoid crashing into a mountainside. So far behind enemy lines, with a bomb that had been invented and designed by Barnes Wallis especially for the purpose, the audacity of the raid was unbelievable.

I was relieved in a way that we hadn't known that the dam was there. I would have felt very uncomfortable about making a special trip to gawp at a place where there had been such a loss of life, although I suppose that we still went to gawp anyway. However, sites such as this do help us to remember the bravery and sacrifice on both sides and are a stark reminder of the grim horror of war. Edersee is also a perfect example of the random nature of 'collateral damage'; the sanitised euphemism for the deaths of ordinary civilians like you or I who have done nothing wrong, but were in the wrong place at the wrong time. Our visit to the dam brought home the strange feeling of being in a country against which our own parents and grandparents had been enemies, fighting in a life or death struggle. Yet throughout our trip, we had met almost nothing but kindness.

...

It was on this walk that I began to understand the reason behind all the geographic disagreements with Mark that had taken place over the last couple of days.

"How was a house in Affoldern flooded by the dam being breached? It is above the dam!" he had said. And "Look, that is the campsite that we were going to stay at just round there."

I felt obliged to reply "No it isn't. The campsite we went to was in Binghausen. It is on entirely the other side of the lake."

"No it isn't"

"Yes it is."

"It's behind you!"

And so the pantomime went on.

It also explained why the campsite at Binghauser turned out to be so awful after all Mark's careful research – and why we could not windsurf on the part of the lake where we were camped...

We drove to the campsite at which he HAD intended to stay. It was above the dam, on entirely the other side of the lake! He had mixed up Binghausen with Bettenhagen. The sad part is that the wind there would have been perfectly clean on laundry day and we would have had direct access to the water. It would have been a classic day's windsurfing.

So, I can share with you the answer to planning the perfect trip. Do loads of careful research, check reviews, select the ideal spot, then go randomly to some campsite barely even in the general area and disagree for several days with your wife on all points of geography!

...

Our visit to Waldeck Castle treated us to a Lancaster's-eye view of the Eder dam. Of course, the flight crew wouldn't have been able to see it quite as well as us, because they approached in the dark. Again, the bravery and skill involved left us open-mouthed with awe. In our safe and cossetted lives, it is hard to comprehend that the young crews who had embarked on this mission probably did so in the full knowledge that they were unlikely to survive. Nineteen Lancasters were sent to the German dams. Only eleven returned.

The group of four Lancasters which attacked the Eder dam made eight passes over the dam between them. It was the very last bomb, deployed by Nan Knight, which caused the breach. Knight did make it home, although only two of the four planes in his flight returned.

We found Waldeck castle a bit disappointing. It was over-renovated and had been converted into a hotel. However, the views from the ramparts were spectacular.

There was even a little, old cable car to bring your bike up the hill if you fancied cycling down.

As we walked through the woods, Ruby tried to disguise herself from The Boggles. Her gorgeous, auburn coat blended in perfectly with the leaf litter. We tried to assure her that The Boggles were only harmless sprites with beech-leaf ears who didn't come out in the daytime.

However, the whole area was fairy-tale-ville. Snow White was supposed to be based in Bergfreiheit, a local miners' settlement. The back story to this harks back to 'the good old days.' Children wearing pointed 'protective' caps were used to fetch ore from the local mine. Because of the heavy work, the children remained stunted and stooped, thus begetting the tale of dwarves.

It is always comforting to know that the heart-warming fairy-tale of Snow White and The Seven Dwarves has its origins in child labour!

16

"DOGS OFF THE LEAD VILL BE SHOT!" – HAINICH NATIONAL PARK

On the Look Out for The Looters

"We're going to Hainault National Park!" That was what I had been telling everyone, 'cos that's what Mark had told me. "It's the oldest and most unspoilt beech woodland in Germany." I enthused. "It was used as a military area by the Russians and is the largest woodland that is not in any commercial use. But it's odd that it's got the same name as a suburb of North East London..."

To be fair to me, Hainault DOES have its own forest - and it borders Epping forest. So, it is very foresty. But you won't find wild cats, canopy tours or any signs of the Red Army occupying Hainault. At least, I don't think so...

It was the prettiest drive that we had done so far, through Hansel & Gretel forests and gorgeous, half-timbered towns.

ON A FEW OF OUR JOURNEYS, we had been blighted by road closures. Once again, several roads were closed completely, so we had to do a couple of U-turns and re-routes; always fun when you are towing a large caravan. Even without the aid of 'German in Three Months' we had seen it so often that we had worked out the German word for 'diversion - Umleitung'. And where there was more than one diversion, we found that it was wise at least to try to follow the miniature and barely visible signs bearing the number of your particular diversion - or go on a magical mystery tour.

The border with the former East Germany came just after a very pretty town called Wanfried, which had a river running through it. There was a very Eastern European looking castle on the hill in the next town and the houses changed immediately and became more square, concrete-y and utilitarian.

Then as we skirted the Hainich (NOT the Hainault) forest, we noticed that the landscape was flat as far as the eye could see. We passed near a place called Spielberg. With my new understanding of German, that means 'Play Mountain' although quite what had happened to Play Mountain in this flat, featureless plain, I could not guess.

The campsite at Hainich, Campingplatz Tor am See, was beautifully kept and the proprietor spoke perfect English. He told us that he had lived in Torquay and then Florida. The site had peaceful little sitting areas dotted around. However, at a cost of €2 per night per dog and advice from the campsite owner that "Dogs off the lead vill be shot" we decided to move on the following day. (I read later that dogs were not allowed off lead in any woodland in the whole area of Thuringia.)

Luckily it was very windy as the temperature was 36ºC. To add to the mood that evening, we heard an air-raid siren and shots were fired.

We hoped that it wasn't the Luftwaffe strafing unrestrained canines in the National Park...

...

"HALLO! WOULD YOU LIKE THESE?" A Dutch lady appeared at our caravan window the following morning and handed us some tourist brochures for Hainich. Amid a cacophony of barking from The Fab Four, she managed to explain "We are here for the Looters." Visions of smugglers and pirates passed before my eyes. "It is the 500th Anniversary of Martin Looter. A lot of Dutch people come here for that." I hadn't realised that Martin Luther had been ordained in nearby Erfurt.

As we left, we were at the mercy of road closures once again. We drove via Erfurt, which was full of drab, grey concrete tower blocks. We were a whisper away from Weimar, from which originated a Republic and the lovely, seal-coloured Weimaraner dogs.

The landscape was amazing – I have quite honestly never seen anywhere so expansively flat. Mark and I remarked that this was where Geography and History came together. It was very easy to see how Germany's destiny had been tied in with the landscape to the east. With no natural barriers - mountains or large rivers - to hinder an invasion, it was not hard to understand how the landscape had enabled the Russian incursion so far into Germany.

We followed the wide, pale-blue skies through golden fields on some gorgeous, cobbled roads. The shiny, square, charcoal-coloured stones were arranged in swirling patterns and the roads were bordered by short, bright green, lollipop-shaped trees. Then, we finally rocked up in a little piece of heaven.

It had taken some grit and three hours to cover the 60 miles to get there:

"20 miles ago, we were 12 miles away. Do you think the whole area is just closed?" Mark had asked before stating "If there's another road closure, I'm going straight to Colditz..."

I said that I had been rather looking forward to the little campsite by the river. When we encountered the next road closure, I managed to persuade Mark to carry on. I was so glad that I did. We wound up in a tiny little campsite, Camping Outtour. It was right on the banks of the river Unstrut with a walk to a castle straight from site. It was just our kind of place.

The owners ran a canoe business and I was really excited about the thought of taking the dogs on the river through the beautiful National Park, which was in the process of being accepted for UNESCO status. There were medieval villages to visit as well as it being a big wine area. We had already seen most of the surroundings. Due to the omnipresent road closures, we had approached it via three sides of a square!

Unfortunately, this was the last stand of Jean's Reefs – the flip flop sandals given to me by a friend. I slipped on the hill near reception and the toe post broke. It was a harbinger of things to come.

17

SAALE-UNSTRUT, GERMANY

Pups on SUPs! Experiencing Nature & Discovering History

A fierce thunderstorm overnight gave way to a lovely, hot sunny day. We opted for a paddle upstream on the river Unstrut.

Although the river looked quite fast-flowing, it posed no real problem to paddle against the current on our SUPs. However, we did elect to paddle upstream first, just to make sure that we did conserve enough energy to get us home. We attracted quite an audience as we launched – there was a lovely group of youngsters staying on the campsite, in the care of a long-haired-and-bearded Cool Sir.

We paddled up past the castle, following a kingfisher which skittered up the river like a bolt of shimmering, bright-blue lightning. Mark thought that he saw a turtle or terrapin in the river. He said that it was about the size of a domestic tortoise. When we spoke to some locals later, they told us that it was indeed a turtle. They had once been so common in the river that they could even remember their grandmother cooking turtle for dinner!

We floated effortlessly back downriver, surrounded by iridescent blue dragonflies and damsel flies. It was so quiet, relaxing and serene.

...

"Halle (Saale) is a city in the southern part of the German state Saxony-Anhalt. The Saale-Unstrut region is one of the most beautiful landscapes in Central Germany" the blurb informed us. The area slogan "Experience nature - discovering history" does sum up the landscape of forest, terraced vineyards and orchards, dotted with castles, which stretches along the rivers Saale, Unstrut and Elster. The river valleys of Saale and Ustrut come together at Naumburg, which is home to a spectacular cathedral.

There is some interesting geology in the area, with rocks dating from the Triassic era. The 3,600-year-old artefact the Nebra Sky Disc "one of the most important archaeological finds of the 20th Century" was also discovered locally - and it contains gold from Cornwall! It is on show in the Museum of Prehistory in Halle and is thought to be the earliest known depiction of the universe, featuring the moon, the sun and the Pleiades; the star 'nursery' of the Seven Sisters in the constellation of Taurus.

We're not really ones for sightseeing, but we did decide to visit the town of Freyburg, nicknamed "The Tuscany of the North" because we needed a bank to get some cash.

Freyburg is home to the 11th-century Neuenburg castle, has an association with the founder of modern gymnastics and is also the location of the headquarters of Rotkäppchen-Mumm, one of the world's largest wine companies.

Neuenburg castle was built by Thuringian count Ludvig der Springer to secure his territories in the East, as sister castle Wartburg did in the West. Luther was imprisoned at Wartburg, which is described as "the most quintessential German castle" although when it was built, as castles went in Germany, Neuenburg was one of the biggest and best.

Friedrich Ludwig Jahn, nationalist, patriot and the German "father of gymnastics" founded the Turnverein (gymnastics club) movement in Germany to promote physical and moral wellness – along with the political will to free The Fatherland... Jahn invented the parallel bars, the rings, the balance beams, the horse and the horizontal bar; all of which are now standard equipment in modern gymnastics. Liberal and outspoken, Jahn was often in conflict with the authorities. He was imprisoned, exiled and ended up in Freyburg because he was forbidden to live within ten miles of Berlin.

Jahn was quite a character. He founded a volunteer force in the Prussian army and was often employed in the Secret Service. The Prussians awarded him the Iron Cross for bravery in the wars against Napoleon in 1848. Like former punk rebel Johnny Rotten (John Lydon) of the band 'The Sex Pistols', who ended up doing a TV commercial for Country Life butter, Jahn was eventually absorbed by The System. Not quite selling out by going on "I'm a Celebrity" (although Lydon did quit the TV show in controversy) – in the end Jahn, the agitator, was elected by the district of Naumberg to the German National Parliament!

We enjoyed Freyburg. The castle was well worth a visit; a steep, shady walk up some steps rewarded us with plenty to see and explore. The town was sleepy but very pretty. Nothing much was open, however and we couldn't find a bank. I went into the Tourist Information Office. "Sprechen sie English?" "Nein" "Français?" "Nein" "Italiano?" "Nein" I walked out, none the wiser as to where to find a bank. It was another tale of the unexpected. We had been told "EVERYONE in Germany speaks English!" However, we were discovering that if we wanted to get by, I really was going to have to be a bit more diligent with that 'German in Three Months.'

We went out for an evening paddle on the river and asked the lovely family next door to take some photos. Their daughter Ella was terrified of our cuddly pack of Throat-Tearing Hounds. She retreated to the top of a picnic table when I took tiny, little Lani over to meet her and refused to come down, despite her Mum's encouragement and assurances that Lani was a sweetheart.

The SUP trip proved rather entertaining. Mark decided to throw the ball from the paddle board. Kai leapt after it, then Rosie ran between Mark's legs just as Mark was trying to retrieve both the ball and Kai from the water, so naturally, Mark fell in. Then both Rosie and Kai made a sudden break from board to shore and disappeared. It took some time and a bit of a carry on to get them back aboard.

I think the school kids enjoyed the spectacle, though. With all the iPhones on the scene, there is every chance that our Pups on SUPs are now a German internet sensation!

18

THE COLDITZ STORY

You saw the film; watched the TV Series; played the game; now visit Oflag IV-C with us

Today – we sat in the famous prisoner's courtyard in Colditz Castle that was so familiar from the film, the TV series and the board game that we used to play for hours as kids. To actually visit such an iconic place was undoubtedly one of the most amazing experiences of my life.

It was especially rewarding simply to get to Colditz. After a violent thunderstorm, we were not sure that we would get off our waterlogged grass pitch in Saale-Unstrut. The road to Colditz was closed, of course, so we had yet another 'Umleitung' or diversion - and then the Sat Nav decided that the best route into our campsite at Colditz was to bypass the official campsite entrance, which we failed to see as we drove past. It took us round three sides of a square and tried to approach the rear of the campsite via a woodland footpath. This necessitated a rather interesting and skilful U-turn with pine-needles crunching beneath the caravan's wheels.

They always say, "Don't meet your heroes" and the same could sometimes apply to places that have loomed large in folklore or experience; the reality is often disappointing. On the drive into Colditz, the unmistakable outline of the notorious Colditz Castle, which dominates the skyline of the town, was perhaps even more impressive than we had imagined.

It was a lovely, cool walk from the campsite, winding down through the forest and a dilapidated tier garden to get to the castle.

It was €4 to go in the museum and €9 for a guided tour, but we were a bit late arriving; the pants situation had once again reached 'critical', dictating that we had to do laundry prior to our castle trip. Nevertheless, we got to see quite a lot of the castle for free. There was a huge exhibition about the Polish forces in the war. If ever there was a nation who has had it tough, it is the Poles. They fought valiantly in WWII. Six million Poles were killed - around 20% of the population. 90% of those deaths were due to dreadful mistreatment; prisons, death camps, over-work or starvation. The mighty contribution of the Poles is highlighted by the fact that there are Polish war memorials in around 32 countries. Polish pilots enabled Fighter Command to maintain operational strength through heavy losses during the Battle of Britain, making up 12% of its number. A Polish squadron was the most successful in the Royal Air Force.

However, despite her pivotal role in defeating Nazi Germany, the Allies thanked Poland by gifting her to Russia as part of the post-war peace negotiations. The British Government refused to let Polish soldiers join the Victory Parade for fear of offending The Soviet Union. If that were not bad enough, Polish troops were unable to return to their home country, since they risked being shot or imprisoned as enemies of the new regime. Many members of the Polish home army were imprisoned, tortured or executed as traitors. As a country, Poland was effectively wiped from the map. It took the fall of the Soviet Union, almost 50 years later, before Poland regained her sovereignty. In their suffering, the Poles paid an incalculable price for our freedom.

We owe them a massive debt of gratitude.

...

1000 years of history rest in the walls of Colditz Castle, but the few years of WWII dominate. This is when Colditz became Oflag IV-C, a high-security prison for those Allied Officers who were considered dangerous or who had made repeated attempts to escape. Perhaps because of the nature of its inmates, Colditz did actually have a record number of around thirty successful escape attempts! One of these was by soldier, barrister, MP and Shadow Secretary of State for Northern Ireland, Airey Neave. Although he survived WWII, Neave was murdered by the IRA on the eve of the 1979 General Election, which brought Margaret Thatcher's Conservatives to power.

My favourite exhibit was a collection of watercolours and excerpts from the diary of William Faithfull Anderson, a prisoner-of-war (POW) in Colditz from 1940-1945. It was a delightfully personal story; for example, he related how he had played his oboe while being conducted by flying ace Douglas Bader* during Pat Reid's successful escape attempt. Anderson stopped playing to signal when the sentry reached the right end of his beat. *(Pat Reid's books about his experience in Colditz were the basis of both the Colditz film and TV series.)*

I particularly loved Anderson's painting of the prisoners

relaxing in the courtyard, with laundry, which was quite poignant for us today!

We called Greg, our Best Man from the courtyard of Colditz, since he and Mark had spent many happy hours escaping from Colditz in their youth. We saw a peregrine fly over as we sat and soaked up the atmosphere. We nearly had to escape ourselves, since amid all this fascination, time had got away with us. The castle was closing and we were nearly locked in.

The pups are not experts on advanced aerodynamics, so we decided against a Colditz Cock - the Colditz glider - as our escape strategy. Since they are very good at digging, we made a plan for Five tunnels; to be named Kai, Rosie, Ruby, Lani and Charles Bronson.

It took some time to find the perfect shot of the castle from the pretty town of Colditz and Mark's photo patience was wearing painfully thin. Ironically, one of the best views was to be had from Lidl's car park.

I don't know what it is with Supermarkets and Schlosses, but I rather regretted not photographing the magnificent castle above Lidl Oberwesel on the Rhine. Nevertheless, I did capture a great shot of Neuenburg Castle in Freyburg from Netto!

*DOUGLAS BADER *is a particular inspiration and flying hero of mine. His life story to the end of WWII is chronicled in the book and film 'Reach for the Sky.' Bader's indomitable spirit did not allow the small hindrance of staring death in the face and losing both legs in a pre-war aerobatics accident to cramp his style - either as a very successful wartime fighter pilot or in his many attempts to escape following his capture when forced to ditch behind enemy lines.*

The understated entry in Bader's logbook following the aerobatics crash rather sums up the concept of British stiff upper lip. "Crashed slow rolling near the ground. Bad show."

Cavapoos at Colditz - *We did not do the guided tour as we arrived at a weekend and the tours were all full. I suggest booking at busy times. We were told that dogs were permitted inside the castle and on the guided tour, although there are lots of steps, so make sure that your pooch can cope!*

A Great Escape - *If you fancy spending a night inside Colditz Castle itself, part of the castle is a pet-friendly Youth Hostel!*

19

CONFESSIONS OF A RAILWAY ADDICT –
THE SAXON SWISS NATIONAL PARK

Too much train - there IS such a thing

We had been saying that we would like to get back beside the sea. Well, now we had, albeit around 100-million years too late.

The Sächsische Schweiz (Saxon Swiss) National Park is a Cretaceous sea bed, now turned into a magnificent landscape of sandstone stacks, tors and canyons, punctuated by basalt cones and towers. And, being Germany, just the odd castle. Here and there!

I had been complaining about a lack of German sausage. Never one to have his wife short on sausage, Mark nipped to Netto in Colditz and I received a special delivery of Thueringer Knackers. Made with love and a splendid double entendre by Frau Beuchler, no less.

We drove from Colditz though Waldheim and dropped down to Dresden, capital of the UK's homeland, Saxony. Dresden always reminds me a former boss of mine, Klaus. It was always easy to gauge when Klaus was drunk, because as soon as he reached a certain point of inebriation, he *always* mentioned the war. All conversational roads would eventually lead to the accusation "YOU BOMBED DRESDEN!"

It was easy to see from the extent of the modern buildings on the outskirts just how much of the historic city had been lost in the carpet bombing. But then you could say the same thing about London, Coventry, Southampton, Plymouth and so many other British cities, whose architectural history was levelled during the war. Klaus' beef about Dresden was that it was a beautiful city; that it wasn't a centre of industry; the purpose of the bombing had been to devastate morale.

I did a few career-limiting things during my time working with Klaus, although I never did challenge him with "When YOU bombed Coventry, you invented a whole new German and English verb to describe annihilation; 'to Coventrate!'" While Coventry WAS an industrial centre, the shattering of British morale was the central objective behind the complete desolation of Coventry.

Jackie's Swift Guide to Career Limitation: Unless you are planning to take 'maternity leave' from your job to travel around the world, I suggest not getting 200 delegates in an International Meeting to raise their glasses to a toast that you propose in honour of a newly-promoted senior manager from Wales. At least not when the toast you propose is "A***holes to Welshmen!" spoken in Welsh.

Two people in the room understood the words. One was utterly delighted with the reaction as everyone raised their glasses, thinking that the offering of a toast in his native language was a gesture of respect. The other was beside himself with FURY... Guess which one thought; "Education in Wales can really pay dividends." I had learned the phrase from locals, who frequently greeted students with such charming epithets, albeit aimed at the English. Cheers!

...

'Casey Jones' was my favourite TV program when I was three. I know that I was three, because the theme tune was my song of choice in my pushchair. However, I sang it only to please myself and reverted to staring ahead and uttering a monotonous "Uhhhhhhhhh" sound at the approach of any stranger. My trilling tended along the lines of "Casey Jones, Steamin' and a...Uhhhhhhhhhhhhhhhh... Casey...Uhhhhhh-hhhh etc" depending on the frequency of passers-by.

Then, if they stopped to peer in at me, my Gran would say "She's just turned three!" This is my earliest memory and my Grandmother's words are how I am sure that I was three. Although maybe I was ten and Nan used 'Three' as an explanation for my moronic staring into the distance and inability to embrace coherent speech.

I don't know where my fascination for steam-train based tales of heroism and derring do came from at such a tender age. Perhaps the relief of Casey stopping the runaway trains and an early affection for those little machines with a see-saw handle in the middle that two people must pump along the tracks.

But I love trains. I grew up in an era when the career of choice for most little boys (and a consideration for this strange little girl – if International Toastmaster was out of the question) was to be a train driver. Railways were still romantic. I was taken to see The Flying Scotsman fly through Preston Station; marvelled at the Sir Nigel Gresley steaming up the Settle to Carlisle line and at home, I always favoured drinking tea from a mug picturing Nige's pretty, blue sister train, Mallard. To this day, Mallard remains the holder of the 126mph steam speed record.

There is plenty in the Saxon Swiss National Park to

entertain a train addict. There is a light railway museum; a model railway museum in Sebnitz; the Saxon Semmering-nahn – a 30-minute trip on a 100-year-old track through 7 tunnels and over 27 bridges; a narrow-gauge railway; several model railways and my favourite, the Gartenbahnstubl in Stolpen. Each table has a replica station where a model train stops to take your order then a couple of laps later, delivers your drink. When it comes to settling the bill, the Conductor comes along with his bag and money changer.

I s'pose I should have been happy, then, at the Camping Am Treidlerweg, to be a matter of feet from the main railway line along the river Elbe.

We sat in the caravan, nearly bounced out of our seats by freight trains thundering by. "I'm sure there will be fewer trains overnight..." I optimised. We giggled as we paused 'The Vikings' DVD each time the sound of rape and pillage was drowned out by the seismic shudder of heavy rolling stock. It was like living under the flight path of Concorde, albeit a little more prolonged. When I lived in Twickenham, phone calls, TV viewing and all conversations had to cease twice daily; at 11am and 6pm as Concorde passed over. Here, it was like living with a whole squadron of Concordes!

At 04:00 we were wide awake. We had got used to the protocol; 'beep, beep, beep' as the level crossing gates closed, then either the brief 'swoooosh – clickety clack, clickety clack' of a passenger train or the lengthy, earth-moving rumble of a freighter. We removed two ticks from Ruby and one from Rosie between 04:00 and 04.30 "It's not too bad if they're only every half hour...it gives you a chance to get to sleep before you get woken up again..." but after 4.30, a train came every 5 minutes.

We know. We timed it!

20

"DOGS OFF THE LEAD VILL NOT BE SHOT!" – THE SAXON SWISS NATIONAL PARK

A QUIET site & a walk from Porchdorf

Deemed "One of the most beautiful landscapes in Europe" it confuses most people to learn that, while Saxon Switzerland *IS* in Saxony, it is absolutely *NOWHERE* near Switzerland.

The name was coined by two Swiss artists, Adrian Zing and Anton Graff, who felt that the strange landscape near Dresden, in Eastern Germany, reminded them of their homeland. Since it seemed a more romantic title than 'The Heath above Schandau' (*Heide über Schandau*) as part of the area was known, their name stuck – and was even pinched where the Elbe sandstone mountains continue into the Czech Republic, which is now known as Bohemian Switzerland.

So, with all this magnificence of nature to take in, our plan for the day was; 'Find another campsite'!

Although our site, Camping Am Treidlerweg, was right on the banks of the River Elbe, we were also just metres from the main train line and we needed some sleep. We also needed to find out where we could give The Pawsome Four-some a good run off their leads.

We dropped in at the main Tourist Office in Bad Schandau to see what information was available in English. They were very helpful – there is a book by Franziska Rößner about walks with dogs in the National Park, but it was only in German and remained, as yet, beyond my 'German in Three Months' capabilities.

The lady kindly photocopied the front page; an excellent informatic showing lead-free walks and detailing for each whether there was shade, steeps/steps/ladders to negotiate and if water was available along the route. The lady also marked out on our tourist map the areas both within and outside the boundaries of the National Park where we could take the pups off lead. With a grin, she assured me that, unlike in the Hainich National Park, "Dogs off the lead vill NOT be shot!"

We found a campsite at Gohrisch, which was once the home of the composer Dimitri Schostakowitsch. Gohrisch is a pretty, touristy village just outside the boundaries of the National Park, so there was plenty of scope for off-lead walking, but the campsite was full until the end of the month! We drove to what had been our original choice of campsite, Camping Entenfarm (The Duck Farm) near Hohnstein and realised that we had found home. We had been on our way there, but had been dazzled by Am Treidlerweg's proximity to the river Elbe. Why oh why had we not gone there in the first place?

Hohnstein is one of the areas where dogs can walk off lead and the drive there on the north side of the river Elbe was stunning; a twisting ascent through gnarled and ancient beech forests. The campsite was verdant and tranquil and the lady running it was extremely friendly. We told her that we would arrive the following day with the caravan between ten and twelve.

So, we fabricated a cunning plan for the next few days. We collated all our tourist information and checked the lead-free walks. Julia Bradbury did one of her 'German Wanderlust' walks in the area and we had figured out our own route, which took in most of the 'must see' sights and rock formations. The famous long-distance circular footpath, the Malerweg, or 'Painters Way' through the National Park had several sections on which dogs could walk off lead.

For now, however, we walked the dogs up the river Elbe again from the campsite Am Treidlerweg and waved at the paddle steamers. "Sunday night. There should be fewer trains..." we reassured ourselves. We don't know if there were. Luckily, it was cooler, so we closed all windows and vents in the caravan and found that ear plugs really helped.

The following morning, as we packed up, we spoke the international language of music. The chap opposite had 'AC/DC' emblazoned on the tank of his motorbike.

"AC/DC was the first band I ever saw live!" I told him.

"When?" He asked.

"1978." I replied.

"Ah, Bon Scott!" he replied. Instant friendship!

(Bon Scott was the ill-fated lead singer who died in February 1980, aged 33. Scott was replaced by Brian Johnson of the UK band 'Geordie'. Johnson apparently impressed Aussie band AC/DC when they went to see him perform; not only with his gravelly vocals but his encore, which involved him writhing around on stage screaming. It turned out later that this was due to an attack of appendicitis. Rock and Roll!)

Germany is certainly the place to come if you like retro rock music. A Richie Blackmore concert was advertised in Rothenberg ob der Tauber and Alice Cooper was performing with Deep Purple in Dresden. Unfortunately, not until November – 'else I might have re-visited my Rock Chick Roots!

...

We were up and away and had pitched at Campingplatz Entenfarm by around 11:30 in a green and peaceful area. Not a train to be heard. In fact, there was nothing to be heard! That was MUCH more like it.

We had a relaxed afternoon and then when it had cooled down a little, we did a walk locally. We parked at Porchdorf and took a Waldweg (forest walk) 'Polenztalweg' towards Waltersdorfer Muhl (Mill) where we crossed the river and walked back along the other side. It is not one of the big walks; you won't find it given any particular mention in a guide book, but I am unbelievably glad that we did it. It was so utterly beautiful that it made our spirits soar.

We walked into the dappled light of a beech wood, with sandstone bastions hidden in the trees. A magical coloured river flowed in the bottom of the valley, since the stream was followed by banks of yellow and pink flowers. The water was made to glitter and sparkle by shafts of sunlight dancing through the trees. The mossy shade was welcome from the 30ºC heat. If this was just a 'nothing' walk, we couldn't wait for the main event that we had planned for tomorrow!

Mark and I agreed that the Saxon Swiss National Park was a definite GOB – Get Onyer Bucketlist – and we had seen hardly anything of it yet.

21

"THAT'S NOT THE WAY (TO DO IT!)"

The Unconquered Fortress, The Home of Mr Punch & The Birth of Free Climbing

If you're walkey, climbey, cycley or just love history, nature and great views, I hope that Mark and I have established that the Saxon Swiss National Park is for you.

It is a GOB – Get it Onyer Bucketlist. And if you're not yet convinced – here's some more.

The Saxon Swiss area claims to be the birthplace of free climbing since in 1874, stonemason Otto Ewald Ufer and his companion, H. Frick summited the Mönchstein near Rathen. The area lays claim to the invention of the first climbing shoes, which had hemp soles, the first difficulty scale of I to III and the framing of climbing regulations. *(Free climbing allows the use of ropes and equipment for protection, but not aids to assist the ascent.)*

Although Mark and I persevered for some time with the pursuit of dangling off mountains on ropes, it failed to conquer our fear of heights. Thus, free climbing was no longer for us, although free parking still appealed. We drove around to the car park just beyond Königstein to find that it was a multi-storey and they wanted €8 to park the van (€5.50 for a car). So, we went to Pfaffendorf, where, like the climbing, the parking was free!

Clearly missing the thunder of trains passing every five minutes, Mark hadn't slept particularly well the night before, so we had decided against THE BIG WALK. Today, our objective was to storm the magnificent fortress above Königstein.

We followed various footpaths and did a cool, beechy descent from Pfaffendorf to the town of Königstein, followed by a sporting climb back uphill to the Königstein fortress. We chose one of the non-route-marked paths. There were beautiful, mossy sandstone boulders and sandstone stacks hidden in the woods as well as a fair few nettles - but the up side was that we had it all to ourselves!

Festung Königstein is one of the largest mountain fortresses in Europe and it is impressive how it is almost embedded into the rock. Visible for miles, sitting on top of a table mountain at a height of 247-metres, it comes as no surprise that it was never conquered.

It did not conquer our hearts, however. It was all a bit commercial. It had been rebuilt in recent years and its shiny, new battlements were under assault by droves of people, waddling up from the multi-storey car park on foot or riding the short distance in gaudy little leisure trains.

We decided against the €10 each entry fee and simply walked around the perimeter, drinking in the majestic vistas, which swept down to the River Elbe.

We still commented that these were still just the 'B' list walks. They were beautiful – and since we were outside the National Park, our pups could run free. We met a lovely German family and although the sign said 'No Dogs

Allowed' on the Panorama Lift up the outside of the fortress, they told us that they had just been up the lift with their dog, who had also been permitted inside the castle.

On our ascent back up to Pfaffendorf, my sandal broke! That was two pairs of sandals in two weeks – and now I had none left. (I probably shouldn't do such rough walks in sandals.) The weather indicated a wet day coming, so I suggested going into Dresden to look for sandals. Then I thought 'Amazon'. Thank goodness for Amazon. I ordered an identical pair of sandals, which were delivered to the Post Office in Hohnstein two days later, thus averting any need to schlep around a Big Bad City in a vain search for suitable footwear!

It rained hard overnight, which necessitated the reconstruction of the paddle vaulting in the awning. After the strenuous walk to Festung Königstein, we decided to take it easy and potter over to Hohnstein, rather than doing THE BIG WALK.

I hate shoes! I had no choice but to wear my trainers, since now all me sandals had broken. I was sure that my feet had spread as a result of my 2-year sandal-wearing habit. My trainers, which used to slide on like a comfy pair of slippers, made my feet feel like they had gone to Japan to be bound.

We set off up the little road to the side of Campsite Entenfarm and joined a bridleway. It was all through open landscape, with beautiful views across golden fields of wheat to shadowy, blue mountains in the distance. It was also quite hot and poor Kai boy was suffering. We kept wetting him down from our water bottles and stopped to rest frequently in whatever shade we could find.

We could see little sign of civilisation anywhere and just as I said, "Where is this town?" guess what hove into view. A magnificent, medieval castle on an outcrop of rock with a picture-perfect village below.

We learned that Hohnstein is apparently the home of Mr Punch. German puppeteer, Max Jacob, moved there and developed his Hohnsteiner Kasper, the German equivalent of Punch and Judy.

We wandered down cobbled streets to the centre, admiring the Town Hall, which is the oldest timber building in the town. We relaxed in the shade and enjoyed a coffee and a pancake with ice cream while watching the world go by. All for €8!

To get back, we worked out that we needed to follow the paths marked by the green line on the white background. We wound past steep sandstone escarpments in the welcome shade of the forest. We were treated to select glimpses of the castle at Hohnstein between the trunks. We were in danger of getting neck ache from looking up at the beauty which surrounded us. Since we had strayed back into the National Park, we respected the need to keep the dogs on their leads, but I did wonder if the requirement was as much for the safety of the dogs. Just off the path, there were, in places, some sudden and precipitous drops!

We stopped at the Gautchegrotte – named after Carl Friedrich Constantin Gautche (I don't know who he is either!) It reminded me a little of Mesa Verde in Colorado. There were huge caves, which had formed underneath sandstone overhangs; damp and green, decorated with ferns and mosses. Two German lads joined us. "Awesome!" they exclaimed, speaking our minds for us.

We had been walking for ages and stopped, considering our position, at a signpost which claimed that we were still only 15 minutes from Hohnstein. By our calculation, we should have been nearly home. "Where do you think we are?" we asked each other simultaneously.

A Dutch family wandered up and joined us in our geographic cogitations. "We think we're here" Mark pointed at his map "but we don't know how we've got here!" The Dutch chap looked at his map and we all concurred that we were definitely there, although Mark and I were in the wrong 'there'! "I think this is a new road." The Dutchman said. His map was more detailed than ours.

Then we sussed out that we had made the schoolboy error of following the path marked by the green line on the white background when we should have been following the path marked by an identical green line on a white background, which was very near the path that we were now on. How UTTERLY STUPID of us!

One of the little girls said something in Dutch. "She likes the little black dog!" her mum told me. "Would you like to walk her?" I asked. She readily took Lani's lead and skipped off with a grin from ear to ear. We donated Rosie and Ruby's leads to the two boys and they marched along as happy as Larry. "We were wondering whether to get a dog" Mum said, "but I think they will want three dogs, not one!" We apologised for our bad influence but softened the blow by saying "Three dogs IS easier than one..."

We sat on a shady bench and said our goodbyes. It took some time, as a lot of puppy cuddling went on. We parted ways as we walked back to the Grundmuhl. The family were staying in Camping Königstein, next to Am Treidlerweg, from where we had moved. We asked how they got on with the noise. "We don't hear the trains anymore." They said. "And we like to swim. We swim in the river every day!"

We were relieved to get home – it was nearly 6pm and we had left just after 1. It hadn't been quite the relaxing little stroll that we had intended, but it had been so worth it. "I know I keep saying it" said Mark "but I'm really glad that we went the wrong way!" And do you know what? So am I!

Sometimes wrong helps us find the right. As Mr Punch did say – "That's the way to do it!"

22

SOCIAL SHAME, STORMS & A SITTING

Sold out by my husband!

I shamed myself.

Our German neighbours, Jenny and Marco, had invited us over for a beer before dinner. I took over a couple of bottles of Weißbier. "In plastic bottles? You don't drink beer from plastic bottles! At least not the first beer..." Marco reprimanded me and provided us with 'proper' beer in glass bottles.

He explained the German Purity Laws. "Just three ingredients are allowed in beer. Malt, hops and yeast. And water. Four ingredients." Clearly plastic did not come into it. "I know you bought these in Lidl!" he laughed. Just as I started to try to justify myself, saying that we wanted Weißbier and Lidl only had Weißbier in plastic bottles, Mark decided it was a good time to add that I was formerly a professional beer taster. "YOU WORKED IN A BREWERY AND YOU BOUGHT BEER IN PLASTIC BOTTLES?!" Marco was aghast.

I didn't even know that you could get beer in plastic

bottles. It is typical that the only time that I have EVER bought beer in plastic bottles ended up being the one occasion where not only did I socialise with a connoisseur from a country where beer is a revered National drink, but was sold out by my husband as having a professional palate.

Marco told us that he worked in a kind of Dating Hall in Berlin. "Old people want to have sex too! HOO HA HA!" he chuckled mischievously. The set-up seemed to be a ballroom with old fashioned phones on each table, which enabled potential suitors to ring across to ask someone that they liked the look of to dance. It all sounded very civilised.

Sandra and Christoph from Bavaria joined us as did our other two neighbours from Heidelberg. They were all very sweet, speaking in English for our benefit. Marco told us that Sandra and Christoph had been secretly hankering for a look inside our caravan. I didn't know if this was true; I had an inkling that it might just have been Marco being naughty – or wanting a look himself! Sandra and Christoph looked embarrassed as we told them that they were welcome any time.

Conversation got on to 'The Vikings' TV Series, which we were watching on DVD. Marco shattered my illusions. He told me that gnarly, axe-wielding hero Ragnar Lothbrok used to model underpants for Calvin Klein. He even showed me pictures on his phone. It RUINED it for me!

We crawled home about midnight and wondered what to do with two uncooked trout that we had defrosted for our dinner. We ate a handful of peanuts. Beer and peanuts-for-tea - always the sign of a good night - and put ourselves to bed.

...

We studied a weather map of Europe. The whole of Germany was stricken by storms. There were severe weather warnings; floods and landslides in places – and it was worse in the Czech Republic. We decided to sit tight for a while where we were.

Marco and Jenny came over for a highly prized treat – a cup of 'English Tea', along with their gorgeous little daughter, Anna, who set up her easel. She wanted to paint us, it seemed, as well as Ruby. It ended up being a long sitting, not that we were doing anything else. It poured with rain all day. Jenny and Marco had promised to play Talisman with their boys, Otto and Willy, so they left after tea and a chat, but Anna sat there for hours sketching us then painting us. I couldn't wait to see the finished masterpiece.

Jenny had told us that it was her ambition to come to England and see Stonehenge. We pointed out Stonehenge and Bournemouth, which is where we live when not travelling, on the map.

We told them that we were related. We were all Saxons. Marco agreed "Wessex, Essex, Sussex!" We told him that we lived in Wessex. The flag of Wessex, a gold Wyvern and cross on a red background, is actually based on the ancient West Saxon standard - and was the flag carried into battle by English armies right up until the 15th Century.

The sitting got a little bit cold, but since Anna was so patient, we felt honour-bound not to abandon it. The finished painting was unveiled around 6pm and it was brilliant. Marco told us that Anna wanted us to have it as a gift. We were so touched. She had made a lovely composition of Mark and I sitting together petting Ruby. She captured details of my dress, Mark's shirt and even the colour of the blanket on which we were seated.

The Saxon Swiss National Park has long been a

renowned venue for painters. The 'Malerweg', or 'Painters' Way' is one of the main walking routes through the area. Canaletto visited the area along with many others, so it was lovely and very fitting to have been given such a personal souvenir from a real Maler. Anna's painting was given pride of place in Caravan Kismet - and has since accompanied us on all of our travels.

We did manage to eat yesterday's trout but Anna came over twice to ask if we were coming to visit – and could we bring the dogs? We were shattered after our unaccustomed late night. "Shall I go over and see if we can do a rain check?" Mark asked. He came back and said that they were all ready to receive us and Anna looked desolate that we might not come over. "We will go over for one...!" we agreed.

We were so glad that we did. Marco produced Weißbier "We got this especially for you. From Bavaria!" Christoph leapt up. Marco explained "He is from Bavaria. He says it is a sin to drink Weißbier from the bottle." It seemed that my German beer drinking education was not yet complete. Christoph duly returned with two tall glasses, which looked like they had just been washed up. "The glass have to be wetted with water. Not dry." Marco told us.

Marco then poured the Weißbier. There is a whole art to this. He put the bottle deep inside the glass and upended it vertically. The beer welled up the sides of the glass and around the neck of the bottle. Marco reserved a tiny amount in the bottle, which he then rolled between his hands before dramatically tipping the very last drop from the bottle right in the middle of the head. "It's like sex!" Marco giggled. "You have to get the very last bit out. HOO HA HA!" The head on the Weißbier rose majestically above the rim of the glass and, a thing of beauty, it was ready. "Prost!"

"30-years' experience as a barman." Marco told us. He

explained that the German toast "Prost" is all about trust. The toast is always made one-to-one. "You must look the other person directly in the eye as you toast them. You must never cross over someone offering or accepting a toast in order to toast others. The sloshing of the ale as you clank together your Stein or glass is a further gesture of trust. Some liquid jumps from one Stein to the other – so that if one drink is poisoned, the poison would be transferred."

Christoph and Sandra were leaving for Berlin the following day. Marco handed out tips about his home city and informed us that there is a slang spoken in Berlin but it is banned, because the authorities want 'High German' to be spoken. I told them about Cockney Rhyming Slang and said it was often used by criminals to hide their intentions. Christoph laughed and said that all Berliners were criminals. Marco said that Christoph was a criminal for taking his children away so that Otto, Willy and Anna would have no-one to play with.

We suggested that Marco should tell Christoph and Sandra all about the highlights of Berlin, then give them some photographs to show the people at home. Then, they wouldn't need to leave!

Otto was in a particularly cheeky mood. He came in and announced, "I have to go poop!" complete with squatting action. Anna was again so sweet – she made beds for all the puppies and covered them up with little blankets when they curled up and went to sleep.

Tempting as it was to stay, we did manage to stick to just one beer. It was made up for with the milk of human kindness. Tired or not, it is an important lesson in life to always enjoy what you've got while you have it. It might not come around again.

Although I thought that Mark was in danger of asking to adopt Anna!

23

THE BIG WALK – UTTEWALDER GRUND & BASTEIBRUCKE

A lost world - in more ways than one - as we took in the BEST sights in Saxon Switzerland

TODAY was THE DAY. The weather was right. Everybody was fighting fit. Finally, the time had come. We were going to do THE BIG WALK!

We were lost from even before the outset. We parked at the village of Rathewalde, but I had been so busy repeatedly trying to pronounce Rathewalde properly (Rathe Valda. RaTe Valda. Grrrrat e Valda) en route that I had failed to navigate to the free car park that Marco had told us about, which was a short walk from the village centre.

We paid to park in the village and then started our walk by immediately passing the free car park. Thus, I had efficiently succeeded in annoying Mark on several counts simultaneously!

Almost as soon as we set off, it all got a bit Bear Grylls. Mark checked the map as our path petered out in a forest. We suddenly realised that we were gazing down a precipice. We quickly clipped the dogs on to their leads. Unaided, we had found the quick way to descend into to the Uttewalder Grund...

We backtracked, meeting hordes of other lost souls, most of whom didn't even have maps. We found that we had made the schoolboy error of missing a route-marker that was painted on the wrong side of a tree. We saw it – beautifully clear and evident – as we returned from The Wrong Way!

We had another quick check of the map to identify which precipice we had been staring down. It is always good to pinpoint exactly where you might have stepped into the void to meet your maker. I suspect that the path that we had followed was a track used by rock climbers to exit from the top of a climbing route. It goes to show that just because you can see a clear path, it doesn't mean that it is safe to follow.

We finally descended a rickety, almost vertical staircase and entered the Uttewalder Grund; a secret, damp, green mossy canyon. We felt like we had stepped into Jurassic Park.

The steep, cool gorges generate their own micro climate and are host to many plants that would normally be found at much higher altitude. We passed through a rock arch, which had been the subject for many a painter, then came upon a sign to the Basteibrucke, the famous bridge. We decided that, even though it was very commercial, since we were so close and it was one of THE iconic sights in Saxon Switzerland, it had to be done. It was 6pm and after we had stopped to refuel with a welcome sausage break with stupendous views, the worst of the crowds had dispersed. The Bastei is free to visit, however that is not the only draw. When you see the majestic rock formations and the magical 76.5m stone bridge, it is not hard to see why it has attracted tourists for over 200 years.

Bastei means 'bastion'. The rock formations here formed a natural fortress long before Victorian painters flocked to Saxon Switzerland. Neurathen Castle (Felsenburg Neurathen) was occupied in the Middle Ages. As you walk around, you can still see evidence of rooms hewn into the rock and even a stone shot from a medieval catapult remains.

We negotiated the Felsenburg Neurathen individually, taking turns to hold the dogs. There didn't appear to be a restriction on dogs going in, but much of the fortress tour was on metal walkways and steps, on which our puppies' paddy paws are not too keen.

The current Basteibrucke (Bastei Bridge) was constructed in 1851 to replace an earlier wooden bridge. 200m above the river Elbe, the bridge doesn't lead anywhere, it simply allows tourists to get up close and personal with rock formations created a million years ago by water erosion. A staircase with 487 steps leads up to the bridge. We negotiated this staircase in the correct direction. DOWN!

The whole area is a fantastical landscape, reminiscent of Tolkien's 'Middle Earth.' It came as no surprise to find that parts of the 'Narnia' films were filmed here.

The views were to die for in every direction. From the Bastei, there is a jaw dropping vista of the impressive Schrammsteine, a ridge of jagged, rocky mountains.

On the descent, we also caught a few little glances across to the table mountains of Lilienstein, Pfaffenstein and Königstein, all cradled by a bend of the River Elbe.

Our return took us via the Amselsee Lake and Amselfall waterfall. Amselsee is also a little commercial, but in the stillness of the early evening, the kiosks were all closed. It was tranquil and we had it almost to ourselves. That more than made up for not being able to buy an ice cream!

I rather wish I had taken a photo of Amselfall. The famous waterfall was barely a dribble. We also passed the natural, rock, open-air theatre at Rathen. Ratten. Grrrr-aten.

We followed the route back to our starting point at Rathewalde. Rathe Valda. RaTe Valda. Grrrrat e Valda.

The final fling of our route took us through Rathelmuhl. Ratel Muhl. Grrratel Mule – where even the mill itself had beautiful, stained glass windows. Which brought us right back to where we started, Grrrrat e Valda.

And as you can see, after all that walking and practice, I had that pronunciation NAILED!

I just can't imagine why Mark was so interested a man shed that we passed near the mill...

...

A route plan for a version of our walk from a different starting point, at Rathen (Grrr-aten) is designated 'The Golden Triangle' on the official Saxon Swiss website, since it takes in many of the main attractions.

Our walk took in some of the sights of one of Julia Bradbury's 'German Wanderlust' walks. Julia's Verdict on Saxon Switzerland: "I'm already thinking that for UK walkers at least, this might just be Germany's best kept secret."

A GOB – see! What did we tell you?

24

NAKED IN THE POLENZTAL – OUR LAST WALK IN SAXON SWITZERLAND

Lost Again; Collective Nouns & a Fracas with Gravity

08:00 there was a knock at the door.

Today we had planned the last of the GOB (Get Onyer Bucketlist) – our final walk in Saxon Switzerland and Jenny and Marco's son Willy had come to say good morning.

Then Younos came in with his younger brother. Younos was a lovely, clever little lad with black curls, bright eyes and a ready smile. He wanted to know about EVERYTHING. He indicated that he wanted me to explain the electronic controller for the caravan's Alde heating system to him; not straightforward in any language but it presented a particular challenge with a small German child who understood no English!

It took us about two hours to get breakfast as more and more children streamed in. "Ein Hund! Ein Hund!" everybody wanted a dog to sit on them. "Ein Movie! Ein Movie!" Younos and his brothers Abu and Hamza wanted to watch TV. They had watched 'The Golden Compass' in our caravan yesterday. Today, they chose Peter Hart's DVD

'Windsurfing FUNdamentals' ahead of 'Star Wars'. (Well done Peter!) When the RYA windsurfing technique video proved disappointing (sorry Peter!) they wanted Star Wars. Their mum, Ayesha, was not too keen so the vote went up for The Golden Compass. Again. Younos' sister Fatima told us that they didn't have a TV even at home, so despite the lack of language, the kids were enthralled by the animals and special effects on the movie.

When we finally managed to empty the caravan of children, we nipped to Bad Schandau to get a more detailed walking map. That really helped. We got lost MUCH more quickly than before and spent nearly forty minutes trying to work out where the path was that we wanted. We ultimately came to the only possible conclusion. It didn't exist!

The forecast had been good but we had some heavy rain in the morning. It was a lovely walk along the river Polenztal. We had a light shower, but then the sun came out. The dogs loved running in the river. We were in the National Park, so we were being diligent about keeping the dogs on the lead. We met some Germans whose dogs were off the lead. "Es ist OK?" we asked. Those rule-driven Germans told us just to pop the dogs on the lead if we saw a ranger in a green jersey!

To our absolute HORROR, we spotted a group of male naturists walking towards us. Mark mocked me and said that I had been complaining of not having enough German sausage. As Marco had taught us with the toast 'Prost!', we tried to maintain unwavering eye contact as we greeted them on our way past.

We had promised to get back to go out with Marco and Jenny to visit their friend Gurnot at Schmilka. As we got to the end of the path at Gasthaus Polenztal, we decided to return the way we had come. We were running out of time and even with our new, detailed map, we felt that our navigational prowess could not guarantee that we would be back on time if we opted for an alternative route home.

Then it dawned on us that our decision meant treating ourselves to a second, rear view of the naturists. We hurried past, greeting them eye to eye "Hello again!" as we pondered on the correct collective noun for naturists; a 'flab'; a 'wrinkle'; or for male naturists, a 'dangle'? I also wondered about the collective noun – or the correct plural – for penises. In the circumstances, it would certainly not be a 'stand' and in these temperatures, nor would it be a 'shrivel'. Not often one has cause to use the plural – or get the opportunity to see so many together, waving freely in the wind.

As we sat on some steps pondering the map once again and agreeing that the path we had wanted, which would have enabled us to do a circular walk, did NOT exist, the naturists reappeared. "C'mon. Quick!" I said to Mark. We ran up the steps and I went to wait in the shade with the dogs while Mark walked up the road to retrieve the van (there had been no room in the car park). I realised, again to my horror, that I had sat right next to the footpath. Inwardly, I cursed myself for not going to peruse the National Park noticeboard, in German, so that I did not have to smile once again and look them in the eye as they all flolloped past me.

I was having a cuddle with Kai on the sofa when Marco came over and said that we would do a literal rain check on Schmilka. "It will be much nicer tomorrow, in the sunshine." The forecast was poor and we had already had a very heavy shower. Marco reclaimed all his kids from the caravan and we put up the blinds to steal a welcome hour of relaxation and a fix of 'The Vikings'. As soon as Mark took the dogs out, however, the caravan filled with children once again. Some little girls had arrived today. They had all befriended Anna. They all loved dogs. They all came to visit!

After dinner, we joined Marco, Jenny and their new friends Sven and Anka with their daughters Emaly and Sophie. We were polishing off our last bottle of Rhine Dornfelder, which had gone down very well with two massive (and delicious!) steaks from Lidl. Anka said that she was from Freiburg. We asked which Freiburg, as we had come across a few. "Do you mean Freiburg or Freiboorg?" she asked. We said that we hadn't a clue but did establish that she was from the Freiburg near the Alsatian border, not the Freyburg that we visited recently – or any other! She very kindly brought us a bottle of wine from that region, which we were very much looking forward to trying. We also met Leia who was travelling alone and walking in the area. She taught German as a second language to refugees.

Later, I forgot both the laws of gravity and that every action has an equal and opposite reaction. I leaned out of bed to help Kai climb back up after he had got down for a drink of water. As I pushed him up, I fell out. I did a near somersault and landed on my neck. It really hurt. Mark found it most entertaining.

It wasn't the wine, honest!

25

SCHMILKA WITH GURNOT – A LASTING MEMORY OF SAXON SWITZERLAND

"It's not down in any map; true places never are." – Herman Melville

Mark collected eight children when he took out the dogs in the morning - and that was with two of yesterday's missing.

Thankfully, the bin lorry arrived and became a subject of rapt fascination, so we managed to get breakfast.

We were packing away the awning and cleaning but did stop for an extended cuppa with Marco and Jenny – along with their youngest son Willy and a whole posse of little blond girls. Otto, their eldest, came over to try English tea for the first time. We told him that he didn't need to finish it if he didn't like it. He said he liked it - and he did drink the whole cup, so he must have been telling the truth. I think English tea, strong and with milk, is a bit like Welsh lava bread (which is NOT bread – it's a salty, grey-green, gloopy blob of seaweed.) "It's kind of an acquired taste!"

Willy seemed to take a shine to our coasters. They are brightly coloured fruit segments made from silicone. Not only can you crunch them up and they spring back into shape, they stick to the caravan windows. We noticed later that all twelve coasters had vanished. We asked Willy what had happened to them; it turned out that he had posted them all down the back of the sofa into the heating vents! This is a gap just large enough to consume small objects, such as a coaster or indeed, a mobile phone, but just small enough to resist the entry of a retrieving hand. We decided that getting those back out again should prove to be an interesting task. Marco looked stern and told us not to laugh, because Willy had been naughty, but it was very difficult not to.

We managed to get our jobs done in between a succession of small visitors trooping in and out of the caravan. They seemed to find the shower, the cupboards, the fridge and toilet an endless source of fascination. Each visitor returned with a huddle of curious friends and apparently every child on the campsite was talking about "The English".

We left for our postponed visit to Marco's special place, Schmilka, around 4pm in Marco's car with Willy and Jenny. Anna and Otto wanted to stay and play with their new friends. I was amazed at the drive up the steep, narrow cobbled street of Schmilka, past the brewery and under a lovely, stone arch.

Marco was equally amazed when the group of male naturists whom we had kept meeting on our walk yesterday *cycled* past us. Walking is one thing, but I admired their, er, well you know – at taking part in a sport with a reputation for chafing, even when clothed. Marco cheered them on. "Nakt!" he shouted, as if they didn't know.

I mentioned earlier that peanuts-for-tea has been a feature of some of the best nights of my life. This was one of them. We always say that you get the face you deserve;

Gurnot had a lovely face. He looked like a man at one with the world. He ran Bergfriede; a selection of budget hikers' rooms and a little café in Schmilka. Marco told us "He looks like a poor man. He drives a poor car. But he owns most of the village!" Mind you, when they told me that a large house on the hill sold last year for only €50,000, it was once again my turn to be amazed. We have spent too much time embroiled with the inflated property prices in the South of England. Our guess at the price of the lovely, rambling mountain villa in the middle of a National Park with far-reaching views of nature had come in at a cool £1.5 million!

We had our first beer then Marco asked if he and I could change places. "I always sit there. It's tradition!" he said. Marco liked to look up the path and engage with every hiker returning from Groser Winterburg. Soon, we had gathered a little group. The first to join us were Peter and Suzanne from Hanover. Peter was tall, thin and laconic. He had a shock of dark hair which flopped around a face that was creased, lined and looked very much lived in. He looked shattered and lounged like a Roman, limp-wristedly smoking roll ups while he quizzed us about Brexit. "Why do you English always have to have special treatment? Do you English not like Europeans?" he asked. I explained that we love Europeans, but we don't like Brussels.

Peter asked where we lived in the UK. "Bournemouth?" He looked confused. Mark drew a triangle in biro on a napkin "This is the UK" he said "Well, the UK IS kind of a triangle..." Mark pinpointed London, Bournemouth and Brighton on the triangle, since Gurnot had spent some time in Brighton.

Soon after, a Russian chap asked to join us. Marco studied closely how he poured his Weißbier. It must have made him nervous; he stopped about half way with a glass full of foam that looked like all it needed was a cherry on top. He was on his way home to St Petersburg after an amazing (and brave) trip around various Stans, (including Afghani-) Armenia, Georgia, Iran, China, Laos, Cambodia and Vietnam. Peter drew a square in biro on a napkin. "This is a map of Russia" he said. Our new friend pinpointed St Petersburg on the square, along with all the best mountains and lakes.

Manuel and his girlfriend from Bologna joined us. While Peter drew a boot on a serviette in biro. Manuel's girlfriend and the Russian chap looked to be getting along just fine. Manuel was a sweetie; "My English is 'ORRIBLE!" he protested. Between us, with my "Poco Italiano" we managed to pinpoint Bologna on Peter's boot and worked out where Manuel was from originally, in the south of Italy, near the heel.

John and his wife and daughters from Cambridge were next. They were quite posh, rather academic and were doing a train trip around the major Eastern European cities; Prague, Berlin, Dresden. They were raving about the galleries in Dresden. "Would you rather be here with mum and dad or at home with your mates?" Mark asked the teenage girls, mischievously. They laughed in reply. John asked how we all knew each other and were amazed that, apart from we four who had known each other for, oooh, less than a week, we had all just met!

Gurnot took a photo of us all to go in his visitors' book, which we all had to fill in. A memory of a wonderfully memorable evening. Something that I think happens rather frequently at Gurnot's place.

One of the absolute joys of travelling is to meet other like-minded souls. There is a whole community of people on the road. I love to share their amazing stories; to become part of theirs and for them to become part of mine.

Jenny and Marco were on a low carb diet – we found it quite comical that their diet did not preclude beer. "There is no sugar in German Beer." Marco told us. "So it is allowed!" Although Marco highly recommended Gurnot's chili con carne and 'English beans', he wouldn't have either when we offered to buy him dinner because "it is not allowed on our diet!"

We were having such a lovely time that we never quite got around to ordering any chili, so that is how this magical evening in the mountains with strangers joined other multi-national nights of good-natured fun like the Luislkellar in Selva and the Irish Pub in Aosta as a classic "Peanuts-for-Tea."

I urge you to go to Schmilka and meet Gurnot. I guarantee that it will be special. It is one of those wonderful places where magic just happens. You will find our photo in the Visitors' Book along with many others – and you never know who you might meet there.

You might even be lucky enough to meet Jenny and Marco!

26

CZECHING IN TO THE CZECH REPUBLIC

We head for Austria – but decide to turn left

Thunderstorms were coming.

We wanted to make good progress south to avoid the adverse weather, so we got up before 7am (eeek!) to pack up.

By 8am, we had ten children in the caravan.

Younos had brought along a friend whom we hadn't even met to have a look around the caravan. They seemed fascinated with the blinds and as fast as I was opening them, they closed them all with a satisfying click. We had to usher them all out and lock the caravan doors. Then, we found Younos in the front seat of the van with his friend, pretending to drive!

Marco wanted a photo of us all together. We assembled various family members and dogs and said the German equivalent of 'Cheese' – "Armeisenscheisse". "Doesn't that mean 'shit'?" I asked Jenny. "Yes" she said, "but you have to smile when you say it."

Then there was the photo of Anna's painting hanging in our caravan. Then we had all the little girls, Sophie, Emalie and Isabelle wanting to hold a dog and have their picture taken, all while we were trying to hitch. Younos followed Mark around, examining the method of retraction of corner steadies and the process of hitching up. Younos leapt into Mark's arms and everyone kissed us goodbye – Ayesha, Fatima, Younos, Abu and Hamza. We got a massive hug from Willy, lots of kisses from Anna and a formal, dignified handshake from Otto.

We nearly drove off without removing the levelling ramp and chocks and as we departed, Jenny ran after us waving our caravan step in the air, shouting "Don't forget this!"

It is funny how you can meet people for such a short time but know that they will be in your heart for ever.

We had been really looking forward to visiting the Czech side of the Saxon Swiss National Park, but we decided that it would not be much fun in the persistent rain and thunderstorms that were forecast.

We wound down the hairpins from Hohnstein, which seemed an unlikely route for a caravan. We remembered to buy our Vignette at the Czech border; it cost around €12 for ten days on the Czech motorways. Marco had warned us to be careful of the speed limits in the Czech Republic. He said that sometimes instead of numbers, they are written as long words that you can't understand and if you are stopped by the police, they impose large fines in Euros. Thankfully, we had the Sat Nav as a back-up, which was very helpful. The speed limits programmed in were not always 100% accurate, but we had no problems.

Our plans changed massively en-route. We had been heading for Austria in general, then decided on Salzburg. We stopped to change over at the wheel and had a brief moment of internet connectivity from our MiFi, which hadn't provided us with internet since Bacharach on the

Rhine. Mark realised that we would pass Český Krumlov, one of the stops that we had forgone because we had stayed longer than planned in Saxony. So, we decided to go there.

That is one of the things that I love about our lifestyle. On a whim, instead of turning right, we can hang a left and go on a whole different adventure!

My stint at the wheel on an unplanned route, which had incorporated a few sudden changes of destination gave me the pleasure of narrow country roads with adverse cambers, hairpins and potholes like you wouldn't believe. It is fair to say that it proved quite testing. I definitely earned my Yorkie bar.

Remarkably, we managed to fill up the Safefill LPG cylinder with our second adapter. It cost a whole €8. We felt quite pleased with ourselves, although stupidly, we had forgotten that the Czech Republic is not in the Euro zone. The currency is still Czech Crowns (Koruna). Most places do accept Euros, although they don't necessarily offer the best exchange rate. The most interesting experience was buying a coffee in the motorway services. It cost €3.33. I had the exact change but they would not accept cents. By pleading ignorance and language issues, I managed to foist €3.50 on them instead of €4 – but they insisted on giving me back small change in Crowns!

...

Camping Paradijs at Český Krumlov was quite simply one of the most beautiful campsites that I have ever seen. It was deep in the woods, surrounded by wildflower meadows and bordered by the river Vltava. We found a pitch right next to the river. As I was out walking the dogs, I met Florian, an Austrian chap with his Greek wife Aleka. I chatted with them for ages and then later, found that they were camped right next to us. They spoke perfect English and invited us for a beer with them around their campfire. Most campsites don't allow camp fires. Camping Paradijs had fire pits all around the campsite; an invitation to enjoy this most primal camping pleasure.

To reciprocate, we got out the red wine that Lars and Anka had given us.

Florian worked for an international company and we discussed how national stereotypes work to an extent. "I love you English. You are so polite! My English colleague is ALWAYS apologising. My Spanish colleague takes ages to get through small talk before he comes to the point, while the Germans and Austrians just launch straight in with no niceties at all!"

Florian had lived for a while in Glasgow, an experience which helped me more than he could know with my German pronunciation. He had been ridiculed when he went into a bar to ask for a pint of Mc Ayvans (Mc Ewans) I mean, how else would you pronounce it?

Aleka said that she had been accused of being rude but said that it was just the Greek way. She did say that she didn't agree with the advice she had been given on a business seminar; "Never apologise. It is a sign of WEAKNESS!"

I told them that they should read the brilliant book "Travels as a Brussels Scout" in which Nick Middleton investigates the truth behind European national stereotypes with frightening accuracy and wonderfully acerbic humour.

Aleka seemed genuinely heartbroken about Brexit. "Europe is France, Germany and Britain!" she lamented. We told them that while we think that Brussels is in no way perfect and needs to change, we thought that Britain's fortunes would be better in Europe and had voted to stay.

Also, for us personally, Brexit would spell an end to the lifestyle that we had worked so hard to achieve. Limits on the amount of time that UK Nationals could spend in Schengen would mean that travelling as we do would no longer be possible after leaving.

Aleka and Florian loved the term "Bucket List." They had not heard it before and I explained that it meant that they had to go to the Saxon Swiss National Park before they kicked the bucket.

We chatted as darkness fell with the river tinkling by, the fire crackling and the sweet smell of woodsmoke curling up into a clear sky that was bright with sparks and stars. Our hearts were warmed.

Just another run-of-the-mill day in the life of a traveller.

27

SOUTH BOHEMIAN RHAPSODY – ČESKÝ KRUMLOV, CZECH REPUBLIC

A medieval gem that should definitely be on your Bucket List!

We caught glimpses of a magical city of spires and terracotta tiles, almost moated by the River Vltava as she nestled into a horseshoe-shaped bend in the river.

We were driving around the ring road looking for parking and worrying, because we had no Czech currency to pay for it.

But Český Krumlov granted us a stay of execution. The car park was pay on exit.

We had decided to get up and at 'em and arrive in Český Krumlov about 9am, before it got too crowded – and hot.

Český Krumlov (*'Czech Krumlov'* – *to distinguish it from Moravský Krumlov in South Moravia*) is a medieval gem. It was given UNESCO World Heritage status alongside Prague. Český Krumlov's castle is second in size only to the one in Prague - and they reckon THAT is only by one square metre! The stunning little town has become known as 'Prague in Miniature' – and in my book, that makes it infinitely preferable.

We walked to the medieval centre through a cool park. Our path was next to the Vltava, the longest river in the Czech Republic, with views across to the church of St Vitus.

We saw a small ginnel or lane going upwards and decided it would be 'interesting'. Gaining height usually yields its rewards and our stroll led us to the castle gardens. Our recompense for the climb was beautiful landscaping and spectacular views over the town.

We crossed the incredible, three-storey, covered Cloak Bridge, which spans the western side of the moat to join the gardens with the castle.

As we dropped back down into town we were against the stream of Japanese tourists, filming every step of their progress uphill with selfie sticks. They all seemed to adore the dogs. We were stopped every few yards for photos. We had arms flung around us, "Cute dogs!" exclaimed and canine cuddles all round; all captured for posterity on mobile phones - while barely breaking stride!

To the Japanese, EVERYTHING seems to be an experience – not to be enjoyed at the time but to be seen through a viewfinder and immortalised on film. With all those hours of footage, I did wonder if *any* of it would *ever* be enjoyed later...

We moseyed through the pretty streets and cooled off the dogs in the river with the magnificent backdrop of the castle. The castle is HUGE, dominating the whole of one side of the town. Sadly, dogs are not allowed inside the castle; it is one of the few that we would have actually paid an entrance fee to explore (and if you go there, you MUST go inside!)

We stopped for a coffee in a shady courtyard of the Egon Schiele Gallery café. We chatted to a Czech / Romanian couple from Brno and Bucharest.

As usual, the conversation concerned Brexit. "Eastern Europeans are worried that they will have to leave Britain." they told us.

"Britain would never do that," we assured them. "but Britain can't officially tell Brussels that. It is a point of negotiation!"

Strangely, we saw them again later paddling down a river in a kayak. The river trips are popular and would be well worth doing. It seems to be the deal to wear fancy dress, or at least a silly hat. We saw one chap in a kilt complete with Tam o' Shanter. There were rafts towing flocks of plastic ducks and inflatable flamingos – one even had a large polar bear tied to its stern!

We had met a sweet Czech couple on the campsite. They loved the dogs and taught us some Czech words. The only word that we could remember was "Ahoy!" for "Hello", which came in very useful for hailing the many rafts and kayaks which passed by our caravan on the river. They told us that Czech beer was the best in the world and that we must try some.

We evacuated town around 13.30. The crowds were not too bad, but it was really hot. We got back to the caravan and found that, although they had moved on, the Czech couple had left a selection of Czech beers on our step for us to try. How very sweet of them! I am sometimes just so moved by the generosity and kindness of strangers. We didn't even know their names.

En route back to the campsite, I had gone to spend the last of our Czech Koruna in Lidl. It was bound to happen. I entered grasping our last Kč note, not bothering to take my handbag. Numbers have never been my forte and unfortunately, I had got my exchange rates horribly wrong. My flawed mathematics convinced me that the 200Kč note that

I brandished was worth about £20. In fact, it was worth around £8.

With only a single till open, a huge queue, non-essential shopping worth about £20 having been scanned and passed through by an uncomprehending Czech cashier who now, quite reasonably expected payment, I had to make a sudden bolt from the checkout to the van to grab Mark's wallet and some Euros to pay for my shop. In the currency liquidation stakes, my efforts were absolutely no help at all.

Ever the one to find a practical solution, Mark carefully worked out the price of the delicious chocolate marzipans that we had been scoffing for the last few days. Ashamed to show my face again in Lidl, I dispatched him to exhaust the last of our Czech currency on chocolate. Which I have to say, was a bit of a result!

During our last night, we had an ENORMOUS storm. We opened the blinds to watch the lightning – it lit up the whole sky so brightly that we couldn't even look at it. Then there was the wind. It was the first time that we had both been truly scared. Although it was for only ten minutes or so, if I were to guess the wind speed, I would place it at around 80mph. The caravan shook as though there was some significant action on the Richter scale. The only saving grace was that, although we were under some trees, they had no large boughs and the wind direction was away from us, so nothing landed on us - and we didn't get blown to Austria.

Surprisingly, the following morning, as well as Caravan Kismet, all tents were intact. As we opened the blinds, we thought that it would not only be Ruby who would pine for the sights and sounds of Camping Paradijs; the woodland and fields of wild flowers, the river rushing past just outside our window. We would miss the night-time crackle and scent of campfires, with sparks and flames dancing up to the stars and the gentle, muted soundscape of guitars and singing from happy, relaxed people.

A little like Rothenburg ob der Tauber, Český Krumlov is a definite GOB – Get Onyer Bucketlist!

28

THERE'S NO WELCOME IN THE HILLSIDES – ALTAUSEE, AUSTRIA

The return of the Small Black Dog; we are evicted from Austria

We would have made good time packing up were it not for Norman the Boreman. An English guy who had travelled in Croatia decided to lecture Mark on what he should do.

While advice about travel in Croatia was useful, since we were planning to go there, being talked at relentlessly while you are trying to get on and being told "You don't want to go there, you want to go here!" was never going to go down well. Norman had been there and my goodness, he had done it ALL.

They say that the definition of a bore is a man who opens his mouth and puts his feats in it. Norman fitted the description perfectly.

We were still in Camping Paradijs in the Czech Republic. After the mega thunderstorm the night before, the power was out and there was no running water in the main block. This made my advice to Mark about disposing of the chemical toilet sooner rather than later quite poignant – and a lot less revolting... Then we set off.

We meandered for miles up the river Vltava in secret forests, through beautiful villages and past fairy-tale castles, watching the rafts and canoes on the river. Every time we said "This MUST be the highest launch point..." we saw more. Boating is clearly a National Pastime. The Czech Republic is beautiful and unspoilt, so it was a stark contrast when we entered Northern Austria, where the scenery changed immediately to a much more open and agricultural aspect.

We drove through Linz, on the Danube, not that anything looked particularly blue or even slightly attractive, apart from the wedding party that we saw, wearing traditional Lederhosen. It wasn't until we started climbing into the mountains at Gmunden that the more traditional Austrian scenery came out of hiding. It was a lovely day to travel. Although it was raining for much of the way, the mountains looked very moody and mysterious, with swathes of mist curling around their contours. Wooden chalets abounded, with one that looked exactly like the chalet on which my Grandma's cuckoo clock was modelled!

We stopped at a couple of campsites at Wolfgangsee. The lake was beautiful, surrounded by dramatic mountains, but as Florian had warned us, it was busy and commercial. The first campsite was full and after a bit of faffing to find it, we went to another. I think I accidentally managed to queue jump, which was amazing for a Brit, obsessed as we are with correct queueing etiquette. I was so uncomfortably close to another couple who came into the tiny reception that we all but mounted each other. It made me panic into engaging the receptionist who had actually been dealing with them before. Even after enduring the trauma of such proximity, however, I refused the campsite's kind offer of €36 without electricity to pitch by a shed. And that was after they had given us a discount for the pooches; the official charge for our fur babies was €3.60 per dog, per night!

While I had been belying my Britishness and queue jumping, Mark had already looked up another site in the mountains, which was much quieter and had spaces. We moved on and, as ever in these situations, were glad that we did. At least initially...

The campsite in Altaussee was gorgeous. I was taken aback at being checked in by a 7-year old, although her English was perfect. I took the hounds for a walk and eventually found the lake, Altausee. It was a bit of a drama as I followed a Forestweg, not realising that it was a road.

I was stooping to pick up a poo when I had to leap up and stand in the middle of the road with my arms outstretched to stop a mad Austrian driver from mowing down the dogs. She drove over the poo, so despite the shock, the up side was that it saved me a jobbie!

It started to rain hard, although I could see that the clear waters of the lake were still very blue. I was not sure that dogs were allowed off the lead; there was a sign in German but I couldn't understand it. No-one said anything, not that there were many people out braving the rain.

I was so glad to get back to the caravan to get warm and dry.

...

Oh dear. Eviction was looming... We had fallen foul of it again. "A small black dog ran across a short expanse of grass to a caravan..."

The warning signs were all there. Literally! While it was a beautiful campsite, we were given a list of 21 rules when we checked in. There were also signs up all around the campsite which banned all kinds of behaviour, including a disturbingly anatomical diagram forbidding you to stand up to pee – even in the Ladies!

So, when the dogs ran back to the caravan after their walk, the conversation with the lady proprietor went thus;

"Vee hef a problem," she said. "Dogs must be on the lead!"

"OK." Mark replied.

"No! It is not OK." She asserted, very sternly and a little too loudly.

"But they just ran back after their walk. They stay on the lead on the campsite."

"Dogs must be on the lead not just on the Kempsite but in the whole of Altausee!" she pronounced.

"OK" agreed Mark.

"NO IT IS NOT OK!" she repeated.

"I meant OK as in...oh whatever. Do you know what? We can do without this. We will leave tomorrow."

"Gut." She replied in the spirit of customer service – and off she stomped.

Thus, my diary entry for Austria was going to be very short. 'Wilkommen in Österreich – Welcome to Austria!' said the sign at the border. It would seem not. Our trip to Salzburg was now off in favour of the Julian Alps in Slovenia.

Which was not too disappointing.

We chatted to a German couple on the campsite who loved Scotland and were keen Caledonian travellers. They had got married in a Scottish castle and instead of champagne, served up their favourite wee dram; 'Aberlour' for the toast. They said that they liked Scotch whiskys, although they were not too keen on the very smoky, peaty 'Islay'.

We told them what had happened with the dogs (their

dog had been off the lead too. Shock! Horror!) and they asked if that was why we were leaving. We said that it was, but we found it funny and weren't going to get upset about it. "But it is not funny!" the man said angrily. He was utterly indignant on our behalf, which was very sweet. Later we saw someone run through the campsite. We should have reported them. Jogging was verboten; Rule 14!

We chatted for a while. One of the chaps was wearing an AC/DC T-shirt. "The first band I ever saw." I volunteered.

"I have seen them 17 times!" he said. "And Motörhead – 11! When did you see them?" he asked.

"1978"

"Ah, Bon Scott. I was born in the DDR (Deutsche Democratic Republic – East Germany) so I couldn't see them until 1991. Bon Scott had died by then."

Once again, the international language of music – and a sharp reminder of how lucky we are to have always enjoyed the freedoms that we take so much for granted in the West.

...

We excelled ourselves – and even my Dad's standards – by not getting out for our main walk until 6pm. It had been such a joy to have reliable internet for the first time for weeks that we had spent time catching up on route planning and other bits and pieces.

Then we drove over to Hallstatt, which is very picturesque and lakey. En route, we saw a man in an Austrian hat with a gun. "That's for shooting dogs off leads..." I was only half joking.

In Hallstat, we found a 'Hundstrand – a Dog Beach'; It had a sign showing a dog off its lead and was a place where Hunde could bathe unmolested in the lake. It also claimed to be a Hund WC; something for which I have never seen a sign before.

Unfortunately, the Hundstrand was just that – a short stretch of beach and grass which was great for a chase, but there was no route to walk around the lake. A British wind-surfer in a blue van, who parked next to us, told us that there was a cycle way that went around the lake further back in town. We managed to park, but by then it was 18:45 and after walking to the road and finding no lake, we decided to give up. We drove back, stopping briefly to take a photo of a band in full National regalia and a pink sunset softening over the limestone mountains.

I did feel a little bit cheated. The landscape was very beautiful, but it was no good if we couldn't let the dogs have a good run. As is so often the case, however, beautiful was a bit commercial and we decided that there would be many other places just as beautiful and, we hoped, a tad more friendly.

Even as we left, I saw whole extra pile of 'Do not...' signs sitting with an electric drill, all ready to be erected around the campsite. I had been worried because it was 11am and I had failed to notice the sign on the reception which said, "Payment is only between the hours of 8:30-10:00."

I did manage to pay out of hours. I think Madam was anxious to see the back of us. She gave us a very cold "Auf Wiedersehen" to send us on our way.

29

ESCAPE FROM AUSTRIA – TO 'THE MOST BEAUTIFUL RIVER IN THE WORLD', SLOVENIA

Overtaken by a bicycle as we tow over the Predel Pass; one of the world's most 'Dangerous Roads'

We were upset to have been booted out of the beautiful mountains in Austria but the moment we entered Slovenia, my jaw dropped. It re-clenched again only as we descended the many vertiginous hairpins of the Predel (or Predil) Pass, which features on the website 'Dangerous Roads'.

As we topped Predel at 1156m (5,285ft), all we could see were the bright, white limestone peaks of the Julian Alps soaring into the air over deep chasms of emerald green, far below. The pyramids were originally faced with limestone so that they shone out in the landscape; this was far more impressive. My camera ran out of battery as I tried in vain to capture the amazing views that greeted every turn.

We had passed through three countries on our journey, slipping briefly back into Italy from Austria to cross into Slovenia. Italy felt like home. For the first time in ages, I could understand the road signs which gave it a lovely, familiar feel. Big Blue did well; there was a definite stench of clutch and brakes during the never-ending descent. We were even overtaken by a bicycle as we wound carefully down from the 1156m summit. We didn't want to impede him; we both agreed – he had EARNED that downhill!

Kamp Soča looked wonderful and inviting; right on the banks of the Soča river and bathed in warm sunshine. The down side was a charge of €3 per night per dog. "You chose to have four dogs. Some people have six children!" the receptionist remonstrated with me when I suggested that he might consider a reduction.

"Dogs don't use the showers." I replied.

Grudgingly, he agreed to discount us for one dog. It made the pitch about €30 per night, which was the top of our budget, but the view and the location really did make it worth it. We could always have been paying €36 per night for a pitch by a shed, with no electric, in the rain at Wolfgangsee, Austria.

I had thought that the scenery in Austria was a 10/10 but Slovenia knocked the spots off it. Austria, your loss was definitely our gain.

The Fab Four and I disappeared for a walk while Mark put up the awning. I left the campsite on an uninviting little track and saw what looked like a dried-up stream bed, which seemed to drop down to the river. Then, as I turned the corner, I thought I had been transported to Paradise. As the track opened out, I was greeted by the deep turquoise waters of the river, bordered by golden shallows and edged with pale beaches and pure white stones. This part of the river emerged from a steep, limestone gorge, which had walls like polished alabaster. The river Soča wages the hefty claim of being 'The Most Beautiful River in the World.' I have seen a few rivers in my time, however, on seeing this spectacle, I was not inclined to disagree.

We had nothing to eat but leftovers. As I returned from doggy walking, I told Mark "I saw a mobile shop. Give me some dosh. Quick!" As I raced back over to the children's play area, the mobile shop had disappeared. I saw Mark look exasperated as he watched it pass our caravan, but then relieved when he saw me in hot pursuit on foot, my shopping bag ballooning in the wake of my hunger-driven velocity. I managed to be first in the queue and bought a few fresh items to brighten up our fine repast of day-old tuna pasta.

The setting sun turned the high peaks of the Julian Alps deep red. We could even see mountain tops through our skylights. I think it would be correct to say that we were rather happy to have made the move.

We always seem to come up trumps when we decide to move on. It could be a lesson in life; 'be brave and have faith – there is almost always something better around the corner!'

30

A PICTURESQUE PET SHOP RUN; KRANJSKA GORA, TRIGLAV & THE VRŠIČ PASS, SLOVENIA

Operation Doggy Dinners – via the Highest Mountain Pass in Slovenia

Bright sunshine lit up the peaks around us, but today was laundry day. We were right out of pants and our cupboards contained significantly less than Old Mother Hubbard's.

The caravan water pump was sounding a little iffy. "We could set up something with a bit of height and siphon the water straight into the washing machine to help save the pump." I suggested.

"The kids over there are carving wood." Mark replied. "I could go over and ask them to carve an aqueduct. Then we could bring hot water direct, all the way from the shower block."

You just don't need that, do you?

We did our shopping in Bovec; a wonderful place. It had the same cool vibe as Paia on the North Shore of Maui, Hawai'i. In Paia, everyone was a chilled-out blond dude with a surfboard under their arm. Bovec was similar, albeit more for earthy mountain types. Everyone had an excess of body hair and was packing a kayak, climbing shoes or a mountain bike.

We got to the supermarket to find that it was closed for lunch. We treated ourselves to a beer while we waited for it to open and caught up on t'internet (our MiFi unit didn't work on the campsite.) Mark tried and failed to order some dog food for delivery. We hadn't broken it to the puppies yet, but we were on our last tin of Rinti and were nearly out of dry food and treats.

"I've bought loads of vegetables and I don't know what they are!" had been the result of one of Mark's shopping expeditions in The Czech Republic.

"What's your menu plan?" I had asked. It was a rhetorical question. I was fully aware of the answer. I knew that he was about to cunningly pass the buck to grant me full responsibility for the correct cooking of the unidentified foodstuffs and their seamless integration into meals.

In Bovec, while my back was turned and my attention distracted by selecting a medley of familiar vegetables, he bought a scary looking fish for dinner from a market stall. Going by its fine set of teeth, had it still been alive, there could have been some conjecture as to who was going to eat whom. We didn't know what it was – but I did good. It was delicious steamed with a bit of mash and pesto.

Despite sustained attempts, we had been unable to order dog food on the internet in Slovenia. The local supermarkets stocked only cheap food, at which our discerning doggies turned up their noses. It would not be the usual reason to visit, but we decided to drive to Kranskja Gora, a larger town, to see if we could get any decent dog food.

We stopped in the outdoor paradise of Kranskja Gora for a coffee with a view of the mighty Triglav, the highest peak in the Julian Alps. We could still only get tins of meat-flavoured water containing a few small pieces of gristle so we decided to go on to Lake Bled to see if we could score some Pedigree Chum.

We might patent 'The Dog Food Run' as a scenic mountain drive. The Vršič Pass, the highest mountain pass in Slovenia, was certainly an interesting route to the pet shop. It has 50 hairpins (the ones they care to mention) at a gradient of up to 14% and reaches a height of 1611m (5,285ft). That is higher than Britain's highest peak, Ben Nevis, which is a puny 1344m (4,409 ft) at the top.

We were glad that we didn't have the caravan in tow. Big Blue was certainly feeling it a bit and, although unlike on the Predel Pass, we weren't overtaken by a bicycle, we did follow one down – and I am not kidding when I say that we couldn't *quite* keep up with him! Like Predel, Vršič also features on the website 'Dangerous Roads.'

We met a couple from Accrington who wanted to drive over the Vršič Pass in their motorhome. We advised them to do a circular tour going up via Predel and back via Vršič. We thought that descending the way that we had just come might burn out their brakes.

We managed to get Royal Canin dog food and some Loo Blue at the Mercator centre in Jesenice, a town near Lake Bled. We also got a Top Tip on the language development front. The girl in the pet shop recommended 'Duolingo' – a free language learning website. I checked it out later. I had to restrain myself from signing up to learn the fantasy languages 'Klingon' (Star Trek) and 'Higher Valerian' (Game of Thrones). However, harnessing the competitiveness and the addictiveness of a computer game, Duolingo rapidly progressed my German to the point of light conversation. I now even know how to describe a monkey sitting on a penguin.

It was getting a bit late to continue to Bled, so we decided to leave that for another day. Mark maintained his form on the exotic shopping front, however. The dogs could now look forward to kangaroo, ostrich and reindeer for dinner.

We couldn't help feeling that it was rather ironic that last year, we hauled around 100kg of dog food and a shipping load of Pedigree Dentastix around France – and then found that we could buy branded dog food *absolutely anywhere*.

This year, we had been wiser and brought less – only to find that our supplies had conveniently run out just as we hit a country where the only choice was cheap food and where Zooplus wouldn't accept online orders with a billing address outside of Slovenia. *(In Germany, we could order from Zooplus but they required payment by Bank Transfer – so we hadn't bothered.)*

Slovenia has only one National Park, Triglav, although it does make up 3% of the country. We asked about rules for dogs in the Tourist Office in Kransjka Gora. They told us that dogs must be on leads throughout the National Park. If they catch you, they don't shoot, but you can be fined quite heavily.

I tried to snap Triglav from the car. Triglav is the highest peak in Slovenia and is a symbol of Slovenian identity. It is also very familiar to me. My brother and sister-in-law climbed it a few years ago. A postcard of its distinctively-shaped peak has adorned my mountain-loving father's mantlepiece ever since.

Until I downloaded the pictures later, I wasn't sure whether I had managed to capture it on film. It would have been embarrassing to have missed an object that is 2864m (9,396ft) high!

WALKS INTO OUR VIEW – SOČA RIVER, SLOVENIA

Two wrongs don't make a right, but two rights do make a left...
Lost again & heading up to a 1222m peak

I love the Ordnance Survey. I learnt to navigate with OS maps and find them brilliantly detailed. However, Slovenian leisure maps could teach even the OS a thing or two. Detailing all the footpaths and cycle ways with itineraries and elevation diagrams – and grading the river for kayakers, we decided that Slovenian maps were brilliant!

Of course, this didn't mean that we failed to get lost...

We set off into the mountains that were visible in the distance from the campsite, following footpath T1. Disappointingly, the path started off up the road, although we soon managed to cut off and walked in woods along the Lepenjika, a tributary of the Soča. We were delighted to find a series of beautiful waterfalls, cascading through the forest. We dipped in our feet; the water was so cold that it was painful. The path was really well marked everywhere that the route was obvious; of course, that changed as soon as the path became more obscure. Naturally, it didn't take us long to get lost. We soon found ourselves following a different river, the Sunik, making an ascent of Zagreben, a 1222m peak. To my horror, after Mark's comments on laundry day, we discovered a wooden aqueduct. I gave him a look that said "Don't say a word..."

We crashed through the forest looking for the path to Dom dr Klementa Juga but gave up and wandered back. We tried to follow footpath T2 on the other side of the river, but that didn't seem to exist. This is what makes map reading so confusing! Before we criticise the OS, we should say that we didn't know how up to date the Slovenian maps were. We suspected that the path had probably been washed away at some time when the river was in flood.

We got back across the bridge with no further ado. The bridges were constructed of rope with wooden slats to walk on. They were very bouncy and the dogs didn't like them. We were not too keen, especially when one of the slats broke under Mark's foot! We had a slight problem when Rosie decided that she needed to be picked up and everyone got in a bit of a kerfuffle. Mark accidentally trod on Kai's tail and Kai shot like a meteor straight off the bridge. Fortunately, he just landed in some soft foliage, but it was a lesson learned about being a bit more organised in such situations.

The bridge out of the campsite was particularly bouncy and people using it were not at all patient. They would push past rather rudely. I would have hated for one of the dogs to be knocked off – the fall would have been very injurious if not fatal, so we made a rule that all puppies would be carried across all bridges.

We finished our walk perfectly properly, with a dip in an ice-cold river. It was positively painful plunging in, but we felt absolutely, tinglingly refreshed as we dried off on a sun-warmed limestone boulder. We even saw some beautiful fish – they may have been marbled trout, a rare species indigenous to this area.

The following day was scorchingly hot, with temperatures in the mid-30°s, so we rested in the shade for the early part of the day. Kai was a little under the weather; he had been sick in the morning and off his food. We put it down to the heat.

As the day cooled, we followed footpath T2. Mark had persuaded me not to bring the camera. The first thing we saw was a field full of beautiful white horses; a couple looked like they might be Lipizzaners, which would fit, since they are bred in Lipica, Slovenia; a few others looked suspiciously like Welsh Mountain Ponies. THEN – we saw a bloke towing a hay wagon with a lawnmower. It was The Money Shot. And I missed it!

We walked out on the hillside and back via the Soča Way. The river was stunning. I had seen precious stones the same colour as the water when we were shopping for my engagement ring. The path took us alongside deep gorges, carved through the limestone and smoothed by the passage of millennia and millions of gallons of water. At one point, there were signs showing how high the waters had risen in various years. The summer river looked benign, but I would love to see it as a roaring torrent, swollen with melt-water.

We whiled away the evening with a couple of cold ones and a chat. The puppies had goose for dinner; they didn't like it as much as kangaroo.

...

We awoke to another scorcher. There was nothing for it but to stay in the shade until about 15.30. Then we walked downstream on the Soča Way to the west. It was just as beautiful as upstream – the water's jewel colours continued to captivate us.

We found a deserted little beach and plunged into the icy waters. I was beginning to rather enjoy my daily ice-cold plunges.

We met a German couple along the way. They told us that Neuschwanstein, the fairy-tale castle in Bavaria that we had really wanted to see, had building work going on and was covered in scaffolding at that time. That encouraged us to make the tough decision not to return through Germany.

It was tougher than you think. It meant that we had to throw away all the plastic bottles and cans that we had saved and transported from Germany, all the way through the Czech Republic, Austria and into Slovenia. Germany is very advanced on the recycling front and has a deposit system for drinks containers. We were writing off €10 in deposits, I'll have you know!

We had our last, freezing dunk in the Soča near the campsite. The backdrop of the mountains looked wonderful.

As we sat and watched the high peaks soften into the sunset with a crescent moon hanging over them, we reflected that we would really miss walking into those views!

32

KRK HERE, STAR DATE 11709.1, ISLAND OF KRK, CROATIA

We pitch up on the Island of Krk, Croatia at the end of the holiday-and-dental-repair-season

We left Slovenia in a thunderstorm and fled to Croatia, seeking sunshine.

As we entered Republika Hrvatska, we speculated as to whether Croatia was pretty. It was hard to tell. The weather hid the scenery most effectively, but if we wanted to while away a rainy day with some cheap dental work, the endless billboards suggested that we had definitely come to the right place. There was a huge tailback coming the opposite way at the border, queueing to come back into Slovenia on the way home to Italy, Germany and Holland. It looked like precipitation had brought an early end to the Croatian holiday-and-dental-repair season.

We ended up on the island of Krk.

"Slovenia was the land of the lonely vowels, but this is the first place we have stayed with NO vowels!" I ventured.

"What about the Ty Gwyn?" Mark replied. It is a lovely pub/hotel in Betws y Coed, Wales. We didn't stay there and it is not a place name, but I was forced to concur that it did lack vowels.

The Croatian coastline driving down to Krk was hideously commercial – boring, high rise hotels bordered a huge scar, which seared through the rock to create the coastal highway. We were a bit worried. There was at least a 10-mile traffic jam leaving the island of Krk – August was over; the madness subsiding. Although not quite. I checked into Premium Camping Resort Krk and they had only two nights available. They were fully booked the following week, which was such a shame when we discovered what they classed as a premium pitch…

The Germans next door helped us to position caravan Kismet after we evicted the Dutch. It was all very good-natured. The Dutch apologised profusely and moved to their correct pitch next door. We amassed quite an audience. I don't think anyone believed that we could be able to get Kismet's 7.3-metre majesty on to the small pitch, with no manoeuvring room.

"You have a motor mover, right?" Not that again.

"Er… no. Mark is confident in his reversing…"

We reversed over the kerb before getting into our final position by hand. It was disappointingly uneventful for our audience. We were not disenchanted with our view, however. We looked out straight over the Adriatic to the little town of Krk in the distance. We could hear waves on the shore, which was just feet from our windows. It was without doubt the best pitch that we had ever had!

We took the dogs for a walk in the woods next to the campsite. The pine forest smelled almost floral; a subtle scent of lilies. The sun came out and started shimmering off the ocean, turning it from an unappealing grey to a most inviting turquoise and blue. Our eyes averted from the ocean as we passed the naturist beach, however.

We struck up a conversation with a windsurfer, Alex, who had come to shore for a rest, just in front of our caravan. He had been struggling around the bay in light wind, which had then suddenly dropped to nothing. I have to say that after three months, the smell of wet neoprene which exuded from Alex really excited me. 25 knots of wind was forecast for the following day. It looked like there might be a chance to get out. Alex said that he would come with us; we agreed to meet after breakfast.

We got out the SUPs after taking the pups for a game of ball on the dog beach. Launching two, large paddle boards and four dogs off a set of algae-covered steps in a swell, while trying not to step on sea urchins went as well as could be expected. We decided to land back on a swimming beach (no dogs allowed!) We deemed the risk of admonishment from all the people who had been photographing the pups on SUPs in their brightly coloured life-jackets to be much lower than running the gauntlet of the slippery steps and sea urchins as a take-out.

The sounds of the evening drifted over us with the fragrance of the forest next door. The gentle waves of the Adriatic lapped peacefully against the rocks and almost covered the faint background of terrible resort entertainment. We concurred that it was a band, not karaoke, although the vocals were almost that bad. The mangled strains of 'Crazy Little Thing Called Love' and 'You Gotta Have Face' (that's how they pronounced it) reached us through the soft night.

We closed the roof lights and got peace.

Krk Out.

33

KRK TO ENTERPRISE – & NAUGHTY, NAKED NUDITY! ISLAND OF KRK, CROATIA

Inappropriate behaviour in the altogether!

Krk here.

I had been looking forward to my first windsurf in three months. We all agreed that it was always good to be reminded what it is to be a windsurfer. Alex joined us and we all sat in a van in the rain saying "The wind will get up soon…"

The forecast was 25 knots North Easterly with no rain. The actual was 9 knots South Easterly with rain and thunderstorms. So once again, we found ourselves being REAL WINDSURFERS and not actually doing any windsurfing. Who would be stupid enough to take up a weather-dependent sport?

When the rain cleared, we took the pooches for a walk. The path along the shore presented no choice but to pass right next to the nudist beach. After the rain, the floral scent of the forest was even more heady. We found a deserted little bay. I couldn't afford to soak my last pair of shorts –

yesterday's shorts had not dried out after SUPing – so, since there was no-one around...

It was gorgeous. We played ball with the dogs and swam around in the beautiful, clear water. The Adriatic was a lot balmier than our dips in the glacial Soča River.

However, it really was a day of naughty, naked nudity. As we returned from our private skinny dip, we passed the naturist beach, on which dogs are not allowed. We tend to call Ruby by her pet name – and we always praise good doggie behaviour. It was only as I was doing it that I realised that passing a naturist beach shouting "Booby. BOOBY! – here." and "*Goooood* Puppies!" was probably not 100% appropriate!

Since we could only stay for two nights at Premium Camping Resort Krk, we went to view an alternative; campsite Pila at Punat. I waited in the van with The Pawsome Foursome until Mark came back from reception and announced, "There is good news and bad news. The bad news is that it is not as nice as Krk" – but then, relaxed and rough around the edges is actually a good thing in our book. "And the good news – they have space!"

So, here is the Enterprise. Our move from Camping Krk to Camp Pila was our second shortest journey ever – 4.75 miles. *(The shortest was our first ever journey in caravan Kismet; 1.5-miles from the dealer to site.)* However, although short, this *was* one of the trickiest!

Camp Pila is near Punat, which according to our 'Kite and Windsurfing Guide to Europe' is the best windsurfing spot on Krk. The reason for this is the topography; the North Easterly Bora wind accelerates down the mountains on the mainland and then funnels through the gap between the islands.

Mark demonstrated quite beautifully how the Bora

squeezes through tiny gaps as he tried to reverse Big Blue and Kismet into the most awkward space on the site – because it had the best views.

We had to bypass natural obstacles as well as a massive motorhome overhanging the entrance to the pitch on one side and a tent and the pitch marker on the other. The entrance to the pitch was but millimetres wider than Kismet and there were two trees in the middle of the pitch, just to add to the interest.

We certainly couldn't drive on to the pitch.

"You have a motor mover, right?" That question again.

"Er, no..." we said, before mumbling about Mark's skill at reversing.

Luckily, the German family, whose view and satellite signal we were stealing were very helpful as muscle movers. They said that they had been there for two weeks and no-one had pitched on that spot. I wonder why?

So, we pushed Kismet into position and granted ourselves their fabulous view of the Adriatic!

We continued with the Enterprise theme by building a dry-stone wall, fashioned from a redundant pile of rocks. The aim was Cavapoo Containment. We had tried to build a Rosie-Proof area so that the pups could run around freely outside. As regards the achievement of Rosie-Proofing through the medium of a dry-stone wall – well. Time would tell.

There was a sign just outside the gate of the campsite which pointed towards a dog beach. However, it was MILES away. It was 500m beyond the end of the promenade – and past another naturist beach. Although there were two naked people on the dog beach, we were overcome with modesty and took our dip in public wearing our undies.

Since we had not been enterprising enough to go shopping, we decided to eat out. We had Fish and Chips Croatian style; a fish platter for two, which consisted of the freshest bass, gilthead, langoustine, squid and tuna, served with a sensational view of the sunset from Restaurant Buka. The sunset boasted so many contrasting colours that it caused us to debate whether it was tasteless. It was our first meal out since we had left the UK, so it was a real treat. However, gone are the days when my Mum used to say of Mark and I "You can't get a £5 note between you two!" Now, the degree of separation between Mark and myself is always between one and four Cavapoos.

Camp Pila was less manicured than Camping Krk, but we liked it much more. We couldn't fault Camping Krk – it truly was Five Star, but just not really our kind of place. It was essentially an all-inclusive resort – and even people who were camping dressed for dinner. We had never felt quite relaxed there, although the pitch with its view over the bay to the town of Krk was fabulous.

Pila was more natural and had a laid-back feel. Nevertheless, for the first time since we started our tour, we were feeling like tourists. Croatia is geared up for holidaymakers. The sea front resembled every tacky seaside resort in the world. The promenade was lined by hosts of little kiosk shops selling all manner of brightly coloured plastic tat. We had a bakery next to us, which was open from 07:30 – 23:00, even on Sundays. A bit of a change from Germany where shop opening hours, especially at weekends, were a bit of a law unto themselves. However, there were some lovely little beach bars and restaurants of the type that didn't mind English idiots turning up with four dogs...

And nobody dressed up for dinner.

Krk Out.

34

CAN YOU PERFECT A PUN AT PUNAT? ISLAND OF KRK, CROATIA

Bad puns. It's just how eye roll

We had thought we were going to die last night.

We had both shot out of bed simultaneously at 4am in response to a HUGE crash. There was a heavily-leaning tree above the caravan. Both of us thought that it had come down on us. As it happened, it was just a massive thunder-clap. However, looking at the forecast, more thunderstorms were due.

The German family had gone, so the pitch next door to us was now free and had no potentially unsafe trees on it. We decided to move.

Although it was an even shorter journey than getting to the site from Krk, vacating such a problematic pitch was just as difficult as getting on. Our exit involved a lot of hitching, unhitching, pushing and twisting. I think that Michael, the German owner of the caravan now pitched next to our entrance, was more than a little worried. We scraped past him with literally millimetres to spare.

Having moved back one pitch, we retained a view of the sea and deduced that only a nutter would try to get on our former pitch. In any case, we 'claimed' our previous pitch as a dog run, with cunning Cavapoo Containment fashioned from two bikes, the van, two paddle boards, plastic boxes and a washing line with blankets over it.

Classy!

Then we decided that it was time to address the other issue - the danger of just skinny, without the dipping.

Both having run out of clothes made it laundry day once again. It could have gone better. Mark ran off a full forty litres of precious hot water collected and carried from the shower block because he forgot that he had left on the tap with our portable washing machine set to drain.

We had chosen our pitch carefully; with views out on two sides. This also meant that all passers-by had views IN on two sides. Yesterday, Caravan Kismet had been the star of the show, attracting many an admiring glance. One German chap even threw us a "Nice Van!" as he walked by. Today, our smalls were the star attraction.

"It reminds me of Ely." said Mark. "Maybe we should invest in some joke underwear." Mark was harking back to a day trip to the cathedral at Ely. On leaving the car park to walk to the cathedral, built by Benedictine Monks whose only concern was to glorify God, all comers were forced to pass a washing line displaying a row of knickers of the most majestic immensity, whose only concern was surely to glorify a backside the size of Cambridgeshire.

...

We could walk from Camp Pila into the town of Punat

along the quay. We ambled through the shady, narrow streets of the old town and declared it "cute". I bought a postcard of the Krk bridge for my Dad. As well as puns and mountains, he loves bridges and had passed this one on a tour when it had just been built in 1980. Then, it was named after President Tito. Since Tito was deposed, it was now simply called 'Most Krk' or 'Krk Bridge.'

Most Krk is a two-span reinforced concrete bridge, which crosses the island of St Marko. The longer span is the second longest concrete arch in the world - and up there among the longest arches of any bridge. I felt that it was a shame that Tito's first name was Josep. A double bridge would just lend itself to being christened Jeff – as in Jeff Bridges.

Didn't like my bridge pun? You'll get over it.

If you did, then as the bridge said to its arches, "I am grateful for your support".

...

To Vrh or not to Vrh? That is the question.

Vrh is the high point on the island of Krk - and also appealed to me due to its lack of vowels. We spent an hour looking around in the town of Krk; a gorgeous, medieval city whose narrow, winding streets are well worth a potter. It was very hot, so we got a few looks when we immersed the dogs in the sea on the only bit of beach there. It was s'posed to be dog free, but we had hot dogs. It was an emergency.

A Swiss lady called Jocelyn, whose bicycle tyres we had pumped up when she got stranded with two flats near our caravan, told us that she had been to Baska. She said that it was beautiful to look at, but they had made it into Tourist

Hell. "You could not get another person on the beach! It was 'ice cream; ice cream; ice cream' one after the other. But the nature is beautiful." We decided not to Vrh but to take a chance on the nature. We got more than we bargained for!

We were a little unsure of the way on our beautiful walk around the coastline at Baska, but luckily, we were given directions. From a man wearing nothing but a camera and a pair of sandals. Our route back, a Public Footpath I'll have you know, took us straight along a naturist beach and right through the middle of a naturist camp.

Naturism is BIG in Croatia - in both popularity and dimensions. The majority of the naturists seemed to be German and let's just say that slightness of physique was definitely not a pre-requisite.

The forecast was terrible and everything was closing for the season. We had planned to return to Italy via Lipica in Slovenia. As a horse-lover, it was a dream of mine to visit the famous stud, which breeds the beautiful, white Lipizzaner dressage horses for the Spanish Riding School in Vienna. Even though dogs were allowed on the tour, the forecast for Lipica was 90% rain and thunderstorms. The dogs are terrified of thunder; we doubted that worried woofers and white horses would be a whinnying combination.

So, we decided on a course of action based on departing from a piece of graffiti where a Corvid had dined.

Crow-ate-hia - Goodbye!

I hope you enjoyed my terrible puns at Punat.

My Dad was not entirely innocent. He told me the Serbo Croat word for market. He was making a Trg point.

By way of explanation, 'Trg' is the Serbo Croat word for 'Market' and a Trig Point is a fixed triangulation point, used in surveying projects.

And if you think that someone who makes bad puns should be hung, I disagree. They should be drawn and quoted.

Krk Out.

35

ON GARDA! A MONTH IN A CARAVAN
AT TORBOLE, LAKE GARDA, ITALY

Even getting there required a caravan manoeuvring masterclass...

It was not an uneventful trip. We wouldn't have got to Garda had Mark not delivered a Caravan Manoeuvring Masterclass.

It did look as though we had been wise to chase the sun to Garda. We had fled Croatia in torrential rain and thunder. Other than being evicted from Austria, adverse storm chasing (i.e. running *away* from storms) seemed to have become the main reason for moving on during our travels. Our hasty retreat took us through three countries in thirty minutes – Croatia, Slovenia and Italy.

To my delight, in Serbo Croat, Trieste has no vowels – it just Trst!

An overnight on the empty Campsite Vicenza left us with a question about campsite etiquette. A motorhome arrived after us and, with a whole site to choose from, parked pretty much in our bedroom.

Even without our over-friendly neighbour, our experience of Vicenza was not positive. According to Wikipedia,

Vicenza is "known for the elegant buildings designed by the 16th-century architect Andrea Palladio." However, I walked the dogs from the campsite into a little town that seemed to consist mostly of dull parades of shops and two launderettes.

A path by the river claimed temptingly that it was part of 'The Palladian Trail.' It looked like 'leads off' so we followed it, even though it was rather ugly and overgrown with vile, stinky plants. I told Mark that I didn't need dinner when I got back to the caravan. I had already had my daily protein fix from all the flies that I had swallowed along the riverbank!

As I walked on, I could see the campsite from the river. I couldn't face returning via the gauntlet of flies and triffids, so I clambered off piste to join a road. There, The Fab Four and I enjoyed a pleasant stroll past several scrap yards and a lorry park, all of which were guarded by terrifying dogs. After that, we emerged near the toll station where we had left the Autoroute. Then, it was just a quick walk down the main road, with no footpath and back to the campsite.

Lovely!

Thunderstorms overnight left the area around our caravan step like a mud bath and I couldn't bring myself to use the shower block. All things considered, Vicenza was not the most edifying experience.

But then we dropped into Paradise.

The manoeuvring challenges started first thing. We had to negotiate two 90-degree bends to get Caravan Kismet off the site in Vicenza; I had to hold back a shrubbery to facilitate one of the turns.

Then the Sat Nav sent us down the wrong side of Lake Garda, so we had to perform a U-turn on the narrow, lakeside road. There is, quite literally, nowhere to turn around on the road, which is bordered by steep mountains on one side and the lake on the other.

I thought that we were going to have to travel the full length of the lake to Desenzano before we could turn. However, we found a café with a small car park containing few cars that gave us JUST enough room to reverse our 40-foot length into to make an about turn and get us back on track to Torbole.

The next challenge was entirely our own fault. Caravan Confucius teaches us that one should always scope out a potential pitch before trying to drive the caravan on to it. On this one occasion, we disobeyed that good advice. More fool us. Campsite Maroadi had asked our dimensions and allocated us a pitch that was right next to the lake (hurrah!) although it was somewhat smaller than our 7.3m caravan (booo!) Of course, we didn't find this out until we had negotiated the narrow campsite road, avoiding the protruding bike racks and expensive cars parked in such a way as to make getting around the corners extremely difficult.

So, when we looked doubtfully at the pitch, paced it out and realised that there was absolutely NO WAY that we could get on it, we had to do the same route in reverse – the full length of the campsite. There was also a nifty backward wiggle into a blind dog leg thrown in before we could park somewhere sensible and ask Reception to give us a pitch that was actually large enough to accommodate us.

They did, but even that had its challenges in the form of a leaning olive tree which we had to snuggle up to in order to leave sufficient room to erect our awning.

With all this faffing, it took us a record five hours to get pitched. That was equal to our Personal Best; achieved on our Maiden Voyage, when we had never, ever pitched a caravan before.

We quietly congratulated ourselves on arriving the day after the campsite stopped charging for dogs. What, with a charge of €4 per dog per night... That said, this was the first site that we had encountered anywhere which charged for dogs but did actually offer something in return. They had a doggy spa bathroom with Italian tiles and slate steps leading up to a doggy bath with a shower over the top. It was awesome – and significantly better appointed than the human shower block in Vicenza.

And we were not too disappointed with our view, which was straight over magnificent peaks, rising vertically from the shimmering lake.

36

THE BEST ANNIVERSARY PRESENT EVER! LAKE GARDA, ITALY

How far will Mark go beyond the call of duty to declare his love?

Lake Garda is Italy's largest lake, but that is not the only reason that it is remarkable. The soaring, limestone peaks of the western Brenta Dolomites rise straight out of its crystal waters, but there are no conifers or alpine meadows here.

The lake has a Mediterranean micro-climate, which supports Cyprus and olive groves. Palm and lemon trees grow and since ancient times, vines have been cultivated. These now produce the classic wines of the region; internationally famous reds, such as Valpolicella, Bardolino and Amarone as well as lesser-known whites, such as Lugana and Custoza.

In 2015, the biodiversity of the area led to its designation as a UNESCO Biosphere reserve. You might find lynx and brown bear if you're lucky – and the people in the area have committed to live in harmony with nature.

But while wine, beauty and biodiversity played a part, they were not the real reason behind us being here. The real reason was... WIND!

Lake Garda is a long, narrow channel which connects the lowlands of the River Po with the mountains – and this makes for another wonderful microclimate, namely strong and consistent winds. This is especially the case at the narrow, northern end of the lake, where high mountains create a venturi, which funnels and strengthens the wind.

Garda is a Mecca for wind-based watersports. When we arrived, there were so many sails on the water that we thought that we had been transported to that other Mecca, Maui – or back to Britain in the 1970s. Those heady days when windsurfing was The New Big Thing *(probably The Only Big Thing – other than The Bay City Rollers and Chopper bikes.)*

It was our Wedding Anniversary – and what a way to break our 3-month wind drought.

We had simply shed a B since Croatia and exchanged 'The Bora' for 'The Ora' – not gold, but more precious, rare and sought-after. The Ora is the southerly blow that happens in the afternoons on Lake Garda. It occurs as the air heats up and is pulled along the lake to rise up the mountains. An anabatic wind, if you want to get all meteorological. *(The Pelèr is the northerly wind that happens in the mornings as the cold air tumbles down the mountainside. As a phenomenon, I do love a 'katabatic' wind, but I'm not getting up at 5am to ride one.)*

We gave a mixed account of ourselves; carrying our fully-rigged sails over the bridge from Campsite Maroadi, we had to avoid impatient cyclists (they just COULDN'T wait, even when we had let loads of them pass through before us.)

There seemed to be an Italian tradition of affixing padlocks to the bridge as a sign of unending love and togetherness. Ever the romantic, Mark went one step further for our Anniversary. He wobbled unstably to one side as an impatient cyclist barged past, trying not to let the wind catch his sail. In doing this, he attached *himself* to the bridge by the hook on his windsurfing waist harness. It didn't make for an elegant traverse.

(*Non-windsurfers may not appreciate that to carry a sail safely, you have, at all times, to keep it in a certain orientation to the wind, or bad things happen. However, watching a windsurfer stagger around like a drunk with a sail that has caught the wind is always entertaining to watch. My personal favourite was seeing a fellow windsurfer pinned by his sail to a tree. No trifling matter. The raw power generated by the wind in the sail dictated that he had to be rescued. But it was very funny!*)

We were soon blasting over a surprisingly choppy lake. It had looked like a mirror for the whole of the previous week.

We chased each other across the lake, our boards whooshing as they left turbid, white trails in the clear, blue water. Wind whipped my face and my hair streamed out behind me like a Dacian Draco pennant being galloped into battle. The eerie howl of the Draco's war cry was shouted by the wind as it charged through my rigging.

Droplets in our wakes caught the sun. They glistened and tumbled behind us like showers of sparks. As we ripped our lines and carved our turns, we were treated to different views of the sheer, golden cliffs, which soared in majesty above us and enclosed us in their embrace. All the while, the ruin of the 13th Century Penede Castle looked down like a dark sentinel from its commanding rock spur above Torbole.

We came back to shore, shattered but exhilarated. No words were needed. We had shared an elemental experience. We had ridden on the wings of the wind in the most stunning setting. We gave each other a high five and grinned our way back to the caravan. As we tucked into our Anniversary steak dinner with a glass of Barolo, our cheeks were still burning with sun, wind and joy.

We had never managed to windsurf on our Anniversary before. Last year we had to leave Barbâtre on the Island of Noirmoutier in a 25-knot blast because the campsite closed for the season on that day.

This well and truly made up for it.

I can honestly say that it was the best anniversary present EVER!

37

GALLIVANTING ON GARDA – A FEW OF THE FAB FOUR'S FAVOURITES

Goethe & Galleons; a walk along a 4000-year old road

You are often urged to 'buy local' but on our travels, we have discovered that in terms of maps, that can be a serious problem.

In Monte Rosa, we had to send off to Stamfords of London to get a detailed, topographical map of the area. On Garda, we could get any number of cycling and hiking guide books in German or Italian. Maybe the English versions were just so popular that they sold out...

Nevertheless, we managed to work out a few wonderful walks around Garda and here are a few of The Fab Four's favourites.

...

The Little Valley of Santa Lucia
We parked in Nago, the village just above Torbole and walked through the vineyards.

"Buongiorno!" We hailed a lovely Italian farmer working on the vines. He hailed us back, took out his curved knife and cut us each a bunch of his grapes. He told us that they were Merlot. They were the sweetest and most delicious grapes that I have ever tasted, straight off the vine.

We dropped down to Torbole through some terraced gardens which overlook the lake, before following the 4000-year old Roman Road that winds back up through the olive groves and climbs steeply up the little valley of Santa Lucia.

This road was once the only link between the Alto Adige, Garda and the Po valley. It was wonderful to think whose feet might have trodden on those cobbles. Saints, Kings and armies, all on their way to conquer the fertile Italian plains; for God – or themselves.

Remarkably, to oppose the dominion of the Visconti family over Lake Garda, in 1439 the Venetians carried a whole fleet of galleys through the valley on this road to Torbole.

The walk finished under the ruins of Penede Castle, which overlooks Nago and Torbole. We have trodden this path a number of times. The views never fail to impress and are different every time.

It certainly struck a chord with the poet Goethe, who spent a short time in Torbole. *"The delicious spectacle of Lake Garda, I did not want to miss, and I am delightfully rewarded for my detour."*

...

Limone

.   .   .

THE TOWN of Limone is pretty - and quite limone-y. Lemons were certainly grown there, although so far north, the lemon groves needed seasonal heating and roofs. Lemon growing died out with the unification of Italy and the advent of railways, which were able to bring in fruit from warmer regions further south, such as Sicily.

DESPITE ITS LEMONY ASSOCIATIONS, the name of Limone pre-dates the citrus growing and is simply a consequence of location; Limone derives from a Latin word for 'Boundary' - because it is on one!

We walked around the narrow streets which were jammed with tourists, even though it was out of season. When we'd had enough of that and had availed ourselves of a bite of lunch on the harbour, we wandered up the Torrente Giovanni into the hills – and solitude.

There were stupendous views back down to the lake – and we got to see a lot more of these lake views than we bargained for on the way back to the campsite. The lakeside road back to Torbole was closed. (Note, I say THE road for 'tis the only one!) We had no option but to sit motionless for hours due to an accident. The main annoyance with this was that we could see windsurfers ripping across the lake... We knew that our kit was rigged and ready for action back at the caravan.

On the up side, at least our sails and boards did get wet – we had left them outside and it rained!

...

St Giovanni & La Gallerie della Grand Guerre

We followed the road from Torbole to the Val de Ledro

and parked up in Biacesa. From there, we followed the path up to La Chiesa di St Giovanni. Up being very much the operative word.

It was a beautiful day and despite having climbed the equivalent of a Lake District peak, when we got to St Giovanni's Church, we decided that we hadn't yet walked enough.

We continued to the Gallerie di Guerra – trenches dug by Italian and Austrian troops in the First World War to guard their positions in the mountains. There was an impressive cave dug into the mountain, but we needed a torch in order to look inside. (Note to self for next time!)

We passed a sign saying that the path was for experts only... Mark went ahead to check the route; "It's OK, just don't look right..." he shouted back. The reason was that the path was a knife-edge ridge which swept thousands of feet straight down to lake Garda. The puppy-people seemed fine with it. We had put them on their leads for their safety, although in fact it was a little hair raising being dragged along an arête by four enthusiastic canines!

We met a bloke who told us that his friend's 35kg dog had done a Via Ferrata. (Vie Ferrate or 'Iron Ways' are protected rock-climbing routes. The 'Iron Way' is a fixed cable that you clip on to or safety instead of using a rope. Vie Ferrate originated to facilitate troop movements during the mountain wars.)

We speculated that the wars in these mountains must have been brutal. Not only did someone have to dig the trenches at nearly 1000m of altitude – the soldiers lived up there all year round. We had heard reports that the troops had to stuff their boots with straw or paper to try to keep warm in winter.

We dropped back down into Biacesa and were greeted in

the café by the Via Ferrata Dog Man. It was time for coffee and a cake.

But not too much cake, when one small slice cost €5!

38

ZEN AND THE ART OF CARAVAN MAINTENANCE – FROM GARDA TO GRESSONEY, ITALY

Introducing my fail-safe approach to problem solving

Mark made a sly, nocturnal foray on to the roof of the caravan with a set of clippers.

The following day, we found a note on the caravan requesting our presence at the Campsite Reception. With our history of evictions, we were more than a little worried.

That morning, perplexed neighbours had wondered aloud why we were sneaking around the campsite carrying boxes of olive clippings.

The reason was that our pitch was so tight that the olive tree was rubbing against the caravan. The delightful 'ponk' of olives bouncing off our roof, night and day was comical and exotic. The branches, however, contributed an unrelenting soundtrack in the range of frequencies that set your teeth right on edge; along the lines of fingernails on a blackboard or polystyrene rubbing on glass. So, as covertly as possible, Mark had taken matters into his own clippers.

Thankfully, our summons to Reception was to do with a delivery of dog food.

We were relieved, since we suspected that we had discovered the one, unique scenario where offering an olive branch as a gesture of peace would not have calmed the waters.

Olive-tree-gate over, we still departed from Garda like crooks on the run. En route, we accrued an unpaid motorway toll ticket and struggled to pay for petrol at Pont St Martin. We seemed to have a credit card crisis. None of our plastic fantastic would work.

The drive up the Lys valley with the autumn colours developing was beautiful. It felt like our own. We had come here to ski for several winter seasons. However, it was the first time that we had driven up this road without passing through a cathedral of icicles along the way.

Our campsite, Margherita, in Gressoney St Jean was basic but sweet. We set up the caravan to the background melody of cow bells, which sounded like a free-form hand bell recital. The views up the valley to the Monte Rosa glaciers were stunning.

But our ongoing caravan maintenance problems were still calling for high levels of Zen. Following our service, we found that our dealer had cross-threaded the cap on our Alde heating tank. The Alde tank is in Mark's wardrobe. The problem had come to light at the start of our trip because green ectoplasm had spewed out of the tank over ALL of Mark's clothes. In the steamy heat of a Continental summer, however, we had soon forgotten that as a result, the level of the heating fluid had slipped below the minimum.

Now it was October – and we were camping at 1385m; over 4,500 ft; just a little higher than the summit of Britain's tallest mountain, Ben Nevis. The mountain weather was balmy during the day but turned very cold overnight.

I heard the heating pump click into action during our

first night and leapt out of bed to switch it off. Never one to overreact, I was afraid that with insufficient fluid in the tank, it would blow up.

It was absolutely freezing in the caravan – even the pups were cold and wanted to snuggle under the duvet. We welcomed them in; dogs' body temperature is a toasty 39°C (102.5°F) compared to humans' measly 37°C (99.6°F). Four fur-covered hot water bottles were most welcome.

It was not enough, though. In the wee small hours, we switched on a couple of rings on the stove; one electric, one gas. I didn't want to leave them on all night; in my calm and reasoned way, I was sure that this would blow us up instead – if we hadn't already been suffocated silently in our sleep by Carbon Monoxide.

The blasts of heat generated by quick bursts from the hob were short-lived and soon dissipated through the walls of our tin box. All in all, it made for a very uncomfortable night.

In the morning, as we watched farmers on ponies bringing the sheep down from the hills, I had a mission of my own. To find out what fluid was needed to top up our Alde heating tank – and where to obtain it in a remote mountain village when online ordering was out of the question because none of your credit cards were working.

Thirty years in the corporate world had honed my problem-solving skills, however. When facing insurmountable problems, I have always found it helpful to ask; "What would the Lone Ranger do?"

There was much to-ing and fro-ing on caravan forums;
"Fill it with water."
"DON'T FILL IT WITH WATER!"
"You need special Alde G12 green anti-freeze."

"You can fill it with water but it will dilute the anti-freeze."

"You need distilled water!"

"DON'T USE ANY HOT WATER! The systems are connected!"

We eventually got through to the dealer and were told that we could leave it as it was, since it was an expansion tank. The fluid needed room to expand as it heated up and the level was not too catastrophically low. Mark's clothes, it seemed, had not absorbed a disastrous excess of heating fluid.

The dealer assured us that the Alde central heating was independent of the hot water system, so a whole summer of heating up water would not have damaged the boiler. We asked the dealer to make a note of their advice alongside the complaint that we had lodged after the service and, we suspected, with their other note that we are 'difficult customers' because of all the complaints that we have had to make about things that were not our fault.

With the heating sorted, we had some other important business to attend to. Not the laundry, although that was, as usual, overdue, but buying our seasonal ski passes. Unlike last year, we now knew that buying them before November would earn us €200 without even passing 'Go'. Buying before November would yield €100 discount each.

There was also the unfinished business of Alpenzu.

This was a walk that we had tried to do in the winter but had been thwarted; the sight of a chap coming down in crampons had rattled us a bit – just before we discovered for ourselves that there was *no way* that we would make it up the icy slope in hiking boots – never mind back down again.

The route to Alpenzu is steep and strenuous but shady. It leads to one of the oldest Walser settlements. The local

Walser people are a German-speaking community who originated in the Swiss Valais, from which they take their name.

The village of Alpenzu was first recorded in 1200, although the thirteen traditional wood and stone dwellings that make up the village today date back to 1668. Sitting on a natural rock balcony, the village rewarded our climb with beautiful views of the Monte Rosa massif and the valley below.

Although it was closed now, throughout the summer, the mountain refuge is open, offering drinks, food and accommodation.

Of course, we did the walk in our sandals, but should really have been wearing boots!

On the drive back from our walk to Alpenzu, Big Blue became submerged in a sea of sheep. These were members of a large flock of lop-eared Bergamasca alpine sheep. It was wonderful to see all our little ovine companions being driven along the road, headed by two donkeys and accompanied by a couple of gnarly mountain farmers. A sight probably unchanged in these valleys for generations.

...

WE RETRACED our steps on a couple of our stalwart winter walks. We followed footpath 7 from Staffal up to the hamlet of Cortalys, where we met the summer resident of our favourite house up there. He told us that footpath 7 was dangerous in the winter, because of avalanches, so this winter, maybe we wouldn't walk there quite so often... *(This proved to be good advice. Footpath 7 was actually blocked for the whole of the following winter due to an avalanche so massive that it contained hundreds of fully-grown trees.)*

THE DOGS GOT a bit spooked while we were walking. The silence was punctuated by some deep, mysterious booming sounds. We couldn't see anything, but it was probably avalanches or cracking in the glaciers on the Monte Rosa Massif. It was a very enjoyable walk, with all the larches changing colour around us.

Another of our favourite walks is the Passegiata della Regina – The Queen's Walk. The Passegiata wanders along the side of the valley and was used by Queen Margherita of Savoy to promenade to the village from her summer residence, the fairy-tale Castle Savoia in Gressoney St Jean.

Thus, our time in the Lys Valley passed pleasantly until we woke one morning to see Monte Rosa looking distinctly rosy. The weather was beginning to change. Even in the daytime, temperatures had begun to cool.

Snow was forecast for Monday, so it was time to be a' comin' down the mountain. Adventure Caravanners we may be, but we figured that icy hairpins while towing were best avoided.

It had been great to do our favourite winter walks in sandals.

Next time would be in the snow.

The Credit Card Crisis

The answer to the credit card crisis was that Barclaycard decided to cease its partnership with American Express. On doing this, Barclaycard cancelled all our credit cards – both Barclaycards and Amex cards – and re-issued us with a new Barclaycard each. It was entirely unexpected, since our credit cards were all well within their expiry dates. They were simply stopped and new cards sent in the post, along with an explanation.

Of course, our new cards and the explanation were on a doormat in the UK while we were in Italy with no credit cards. Thankfully, we had a pre-paid Euro currency card which we could top up online and use to withdraw cash and pay at petrol stations. It didn't work in toll booths on the autoroutes, however.

Unexpected fall-out of using the pre-paid card was that our shopping bills didn't seem to add up. We discovered that this was because in a bid to be helpful, the lovely couple in the local supermarket were converting our bills from Euros to Pounds Sterling when we used the card. We didn't notice until we spotted that on all of our shopping, we were being charged a currency conversion commission for Pounds to Euros and back to Pounds again!

39

RIOTS IN CALAIS, TORRENTS ON THE THAMES & THE LONG DRIVE BACK TO LONG PANTS

An uneventful journey home...

"Riot Police have been drafted into Calais because of 'Chaos' with migrants and Operation 'Stack' is in force at Dover."

Up popped the happy news on the internet.

It came from one of the Tabloids, so I took it with a pinch of salt. However, it did still awaken the antennae of angst and definitely got them wagging.

The migrant problem was one of the reasons that we were wary of crossing on The Channel Tunnel. Our spacious, inviting panel van with no windows in it and our homely caravan with its large, external lockers and easy-to-pick locks were replete with hiding places for the enterprising immigrant.

However, we had also heard reports of migrants stopping traffic on the approach to Plan B; the ferry port at Caen. Migrant-free crossing by sea was clearly not all plain sailing either.

I did a fact check on both the Eurotunnel and the UK Government websites. Neither reported any problems at

Calais. The Tabloid Press perhaps forgot to mention that the 'chaos' was partly due to a mass migration OUT of England by spectators for a European football match, the Le Mans Race – and the fact that it was the UK schools' half-term holiday week.

I had forgotten about half-term. Being closer to England, the phone decided that now was the perfect time to alert us to a voicemail that had been left three weeks earlier. It was from the campsite on the River Thames, which we had booked months in advance to accommodate us on our homecoming. The voicemail delivered the good news that we couldn't stay there because the site was flooded.

I called straight back to ask if the weather had improved or if they had any hard-standing pitches available. "We currently have torrential rain and 40-mph winds due to Storm Brian. All the hard standing booked out weeks ago. We rang you straight away and left a message, but you didn't answer..." Of course, now we were struggling to get a hard-standing pitch *ANYWHERE* because it was half-term and every campsite was packed to the gunwales with small people.

...

To mitigate any potential migrant problems at Calais, we spent the night before our Tunnel crossing at Le Touquet, which we felt was a respectable distance away. I asked at the campsite reception if they had heard about any trouble at Calais and they simply looked bemused. They checked the internet and the only stories about migrants at Calais in the French press were very old news indeed. I guess that the British Tabloids just enjoy adding fuel to the fires of UK migrant hysteria.

We had left the Gressoney valley swathed with the beginnings of autumn splendour. Val de Lys is one of those places where Nature seems to say, "Just LOOK what I can DO!" We had our traditional coffee stop back in France, just under the Aguille du Midi and Mont Blanc.

The sun had still been shining in the mountains, but as we entered Northern France, we seemed to have driven straight from our endless summer into the drab, grey, wet of winter. We had moved directly to winter; did not collect €200 and did not pass autumn.

Our alarm had gone off in the dark that morning. Even more depressingly, by next weekend, we would have lost not one but two hours of daylight. Our extra hour of Continental time would evaporate just as the British clocks lost a further hour for daylight saving.

We had allowed ourselves three days to get to Calais but elected to get our heads down and just go as far as we could. It would mean fewer travelling days for the dogs – and the nifty shades of grey which was all that filled our windscreen were not inviting for a stopover anyway. Our heads had been way down – we drove the 616.7 miles to Le Touks in one hit.

With Storm Brian being not the Messiah, but a very naughty storm, I had proffered advice on driving in high winds in answer to questions posted on several caravan forums and on my blog. As windsurfers, we have a special relationship with the capricious wind.

We had checked the forecast, which didn't look too bad but as we approached the coast, we had to cross several viaducts, all of which were preluded by taut and turgid wind socks. I could feel the caravan being buffeted and thought that it would be rather ironic if we were blown over, having dealt out so many 'bon mots' about driving safely in high winds.

We arrived, relieved and safe at Le Touquet, pitched in a record half hour and took The Fab Four for a much-needed leg-stretch on the huge expanse of beach as the sun set.

The next day, it rained and rained and rained and rained. It barely even got light. We walked the dogs on the beach and got thoroughly soaked before we left for The Tunnel. I had put it off as long as I could. Finally, I had to abandon shorts and make the dreaded move into long pants.

Long pants are ever the harbinger of The End. The End of our Endless Summer.

With the deadline of a crossing, we always like to leave ourselves plenty of time and it was a good job. Roadworks had closed the slip road to the Eurotunnel terminal.

We followed the diversion for MILES to Guisnes, but after going around three sides of the terminal, we seemed to be heading away from it. We rang Eurotunnel, only to be told that both slip roads were open. "They're not!" I said, "They are!" they said. "Other people have checked in!" they told me, by way of letting me know that I was stupid.

We followed the diversion again and headed to Guisnes again. We decided that it was clearly the wrong way, ignored the diversion and got ourselves back on the motorway on the opposite carriageway, since the slip road was open in that direction. We got to the terminal and checked in. So, we were not stupid. Just all those other lost-looking cars, caravans and motorhomes that we saw driving towards Guisnes.

And we can also report that, having done a complete circumnavigation of the terminal TWICE; we did not see ONE single migrant. God Bless you, UK Tabloid Press!

Back in Blighty. Back in long pants. I could feel my tan fading with every mile. Within one hour of pitching back in the UK, we had four damp 'n dirty dawgs and I discovered the obvious; sandals are not suitable footwear for walking in waterlogged woodland and fields.

Still, despite the drizzle, we got the awning up. We had bought a Great British fry up, but much as we were looking forward to it, we were too exhausted to cook it.

We demolished a sandwich and a couple of beers.

Then we slept like babes.

We managed to get on to our seasonal pitch at Hunter's Moon C&MC site in Wareham early. It was a relief to have somewhere to pitch that was not waterlogged, albeit with a 100-mile commute to visit Mark's Mum!

40

BACK IN BRITAIN; A FIDOSE OF REALITY

Our home comings are never without incident - & this was our worst yet

Dorset. A county boasting one of the lowest crime rates in the UK. A quiet country walk with the dogs ended with a statement given to the police.

Mark and I have both slithered over the hill into our mid-50s without ever being involved in a fight. "That's nothing!" my friend told me, putting it into context. "I've never rented a video!"

Nevertheless, in a quiet, sleepy area frequented by dog walkers, someone started throwing punches and kicks before pulling a weapon on Mark because our trained therapy dog, Rosie, went near him.

Rosie didn't get too close; she certainly didn't jump up. She did go towards him to say hello because she is friendly, but she is also very smart. We called her but she had already got the message that she was not welcome from the heavily booted foot that lashed out repeatedly towards her head.

I do completely understand that some people are scared of dogs. Having been bitten by a Scottie as a child, my Dad has an almost pathological fear of dogs. This necessitates taking the caravan 'up north' with us as accommodation and The Fab Four staying around the corner with Ant Kath to be spoiled rotten each day when we visit Dad. However, we did feel that an escalation to immediate, armed violence towards the owner of a dog who had effectively just hesitated slightly while walking past was a bit of an overreaction. And if you don't like dogs, why choose to go to a dog-walkers' paradise?

The incident was not without an air of comedy. Mark is 6'6" tall, so there was a cartoon-like quality to the way Mark simply put his hands on the guy's shoulders while an almost epileptic rain of punches and kicks met nothing but mid-air. Thankfully, the metallic-looking pointy weapon thing was dropped somewhere amid the confusion.

Mark is a gentle man, but even had he not been, he still knew better than to do anything by way of retaliation. We have seen too many examples in the news of self-defence being no defence – and hefty prison sentences being handed out to those who fall slightly to the wrong side of 'reasonable force' in the confusion of a sudden and violent, armed attack.

Never one to overreact, I was completely calm in the crisis and helped to get things back under control by screaming, flapping, helping to restrain the assailant by throwing myself over his legs when Mark wrestled him to the ground and shouting "Help!" to two walkers who arrived on the scene at that point and thought that Mark was the bad guy.

I gabbled an explanation and then made my second ever

999 call and phoned the police. The walkers took a photo of our attacker, who, after finally managing to punch Mark in the mouth, accepted that he was outnumbered and went on his merry way, shouting obscenities.

It is fair to say that our homecomings are never straightforward! Usually, we just get fined because of our Master Criminal tendencies towards highway crime (speeding) and inadvertent tax evasion. *(Our latest dastardly speeding offence was for doing 70mph in a 70mph zone. Swiftly relieved of a £100 fine and supplied with 3 penalty points, we can pass on to you that 70mph is illegal on a dual carriageway in a panel van –* **unless** *it has windows, in which case the same body and chassis is classed as a 'people carrier'.)*

This time, by way of variety, we rode the rollercoaster of being the victim in several different scenarios in addition to the assault; namely car trouble, tenant trouble, a boundary dispute, wild weather and a robbery.

Welcome home!

...

Our base was a seasonal pitch at Hunter's Moon near Wareham. We had gone there because we couldn't stay at the site that we had pre-booked near Mark's Mum, since that was flooded.

The 100-mile commute to visit was made all the more pleasing as we walked into her lounge for the first time in a couple of months. It was hard to miss the blank wall of the neighbour's new extension. Erected while we had been away, it was only the two feet over the boundary of Mark's Mum's property.

In between "How was your trip?" and "Are you glad to be

home?" Mark nipped out quietly with a tape measure and a camera to take photos of where the builders had cut away two feet of his Mum's patio and removed part of a raised flower bed.

The Council Planning Office was not sure that the extension was over the boundary. We explained how the patio had been cut away and told them that if the extension had been at the front of the house, it would obscure half of the window. "The boundary could have been in the wrong place!" they assured us, but they did send several planning officers to look.

They um'd and ah'd as they rubbed their chins and marvelled at the huge dormer window on the extension that hadn't been on the plans – and had been absent when Council carried out their final inspection. They noted that, apart from tunnelling underground, the extension exceeded the plans in every dimension. They conceded the *possibility* that boundary *may* have been violated – and that *if* it had, the mutilation of the patio amounted to criminal damage. "We shall take enforcement action!" they assured us. Stupidly, we believed them.

Up until now, relations with the neighbour had been very good. We spoke to him and, all teeth and smiles, he regaled us with the joyful news that he had done nothing wrong. He had built on the party wall line, which was a great benefit to Mark's Mum. With equal delight and equanimity, he informed us we could not only look forward to him installing a brand-new fence – but he was going to pay for it.

We asked him about the written permission from Mark's Mum that he required by law to build on the party wall line. We knew that he did not have it. We suspected that our assertion that his wonderful new fence should definitely

NOT be in line with the extension fell on stony ground. We suspected even more strongly that the stony ground where it fell was two feet over the boundary of my mother-in-law's garden.

On one side, we had the help and support of The Local Authority, which we found out later is like having the hapless progeny of the Keystone Kops and a Muppet in your shield wall. On the other, a neighbour deliberately deaf to reason; perhaps because he lives in an area of burgeoning property prices. Clearly, there was never going to be a simple solution.

However, we left it in the capable hands of the Local Planning Office. They are our representatives and that's their job. Isn't it?

...

Dorset in November once again helped towards acclimatization for our second winter in the Alps. On a walk to Corfe Castle, the freezing wind made my face go numb. We also had a couple of sleepless nights in Wareham where we thought that we were all heading for Kansas, but Caravan Kismet kept herself steady and the awning remained resolutely upright.

We can't say that the windsurfing was quite as successful. Where is the wind when you decide to ride the storm? The howling maelstrom suddenly dropped, leaving Mark struggling with a sinker in no wind. *(A sinker is a small board for sailing in high winds. It can't support your weight unless it is moving very quickly, i.e. planing, like a speed boat on top of the water. Without wind, a windsurfer is like a boat with no motor or rudder – and is completely at the mercy of the sea.)*

I was dog-sitting on the beach, chatting to some friends

when a windsurfing buddy rushed over to tell me "Someone's been washed out of The Run. I think it's Mark!" I was incredulous. Mark is an experienced windsurfer. Only idiots get washed out of The Run. *(And me. Nearly. Once!)*

However, with no wind to power him and a board too small to stand on, the tide had indeed flushed him out of Christchurch Harbour, down the narrow, fast-flowing 'Run' and into the open sea. Once he managed to land, he was forced to do the walk of shame with his kit, back to the car park from Avon Beach.

For the second time in a month, I maintained my icy calm in a crisis. Flapping around on the beach with the dogs I once again watched, helpless and impotent, while Mark did battle. This time swimming hard and towing his board and sail, which acted like a sea anchor, as he made a painfully slow return to shore.

Fortunately, Avon beach was replete with professional windsurfers, all of whom were able to demonstrate impeccably to us how to do it. We all know that windsurfers do it standing up. *(Although not when they are riding a sinker in no wind!)*

We had a Caravan Christmas in exotic Lancashire, visiting my Dad and having lots of very muddy walks with the puppies. "It's rained non-stop since May!" said Mrs D, our lovely hostess at the little campsite in Abbey Village, by way of explanation for the mud.

We walked to the top of Rivington Pike and it was snowing. Again, good practice for Italy in a couple of weeks. We had booked the same apartment as last year in Monte Rosa from January to March, so we would be escaping the winter chill by going somewhere that was really cold.

We put winter tyres on our van, Big Blue, in readiness

for our trip to Italy, although we had a sneaking suspicion that they might come in useful before then.

Then our tenants decided to move out and delayed our departure.

41

BACK IN BRITAIN; A FIDOSE OF REALITY
– PART 2

New Year; new start. But the slings and arrows of outrageous
fortune were not done with us yet...

Confronted by our Fidose of Reality, we felt lucky to have
Ruby and her new confectionary-shaped Christmas toy to
remind us "As you ramble on through life, whatever be your
goal, keep your eye on the doughnut and not on the hole."

Although our returns to the UK are never straightforward, this one had reached an unprecedented zenith of
complexity.

We had only arrived back on British soil in November;
however, by Christmas we had fitted in an assault, a
boundary dispute, wild weather and Mark had been lost
at sea.

But the slings and arrows of outrageous fortune were not
done with us yet. Our Fidose of Reality continued into the
New Year with car trouble, being forced to tow a caravan
through a storm, tenant trouble and a robbery.

On New Year's Day; we were camped by the finish line.
The pups and I sloshed around the expanse of marshland

that now formed the perimeter of Warwick Racecourse and I wished a lady whom I met "Happy New Year!"

"It's my day, isn't it?!" she replied. I hesitated at the peculiar reply, wondering if it was her birthday or she had just won the lottery or something. Then it dawned on me that what she had said was "It's muddy, isn't it?!" in a local Midlands accent.

And then, the white-knuckle ride. We were forced to drive from Warwick to the New Forest in Storm Eleanor. The caravan shook us like peas in a maraca as she was buffeted by 100mph winds. This prepared us both for the ordeal ahead by providing a night completely devoid of sleep. My heart was in my mouth all the way back to the South Coast, but Mark kept his cool in a way that contrasted markedly with his wife's approach to sangfroid.

As windsurfers, we're good at spotting whether we're towing in a head wind (safer) or cross wind (less safe). Mark also has an LGVI lorry licence, so he calmly explained his road positioning to me. He kept to the centre line as lorries came up behind, so that they were pushed over as they went to overtake. He then moved back to the inside of our lane as they passed to give us plenty of space and minimise the shock wave as they went by. It was a relief to know that a turnover is unlikely – although I did witness a caravan rolling on the M27 in a storm during the 1990s, so it is always in my mind.

Of course, we would have preferred not to tow in weather like this. It was entirely contrary to my own very good advice. However, we had no choice but to vacate the site at Warwick because it had closed for the season.

Weather aside, we were also a little perturbed by the fact that during the journey, Big Blue started to lose power without warning. If we coasted on to the hard shoulder and switched off the engine for ten minutes or so, she was all fine and dandy. Until it happened again.

We did arrive safely at Setthorns in the New Forest after a very slow and cautious progress. While Mark set up, I took the pups for a proper 'my day walk' – it was knee deep – and managed to get lost! Thankfully, I found my way back to the caravan just as it was getting dark.

We began to ready Caravan Kismet for winter storage, although even that was not without some drama. I got my arm stuck behind the water heater when I was draining down the water tank. "I'm not joking, Mark. It's really stuck!"

I genuinely thought that I was going to have to call out the emergency services to extricate me. Mark was just as genuine in his contempt for yet another example of his wife's ridiculous antics.

I felt like that bloke who got his arm trapped by a rock when he was climbing solo in America. I loved the title of his book; 'Between a Rock and a Hard Place' but I wasn't about to pay him homage by drinking my own urine and sawing off my arm. I did manage to work my way free, with some wriggling and a look of disdain from Mark that was so withering that I think it allowed my arm simply to shrink itself free!

...

We had booked Big Blue into Halfords first thing to check out the power-loss problem, forgetting, of course, that it was the day we were putting Caravan Kismet into storage.

Mark had originally told me that I had until 2pm to clean and close down the caravan for the winter. Then he rang and said that Halfords couldn't fix the problem, so he'd be back in half an hour and could we leave at 12pm to save paying for a late departure from site. This threw my calm and composed cleansing schedule into ablution apoplexy; half an hour to achieve the remaining 2.5 hours of augmented antisepsis.

Then, once he came back, in a masterful show of efficiency, Mark packed everything away. This included all my tidying tools, which somewhat hampered my efforts in the accelerated ablutions department. The curt, curtailed-cleaning conversations went along the lines of; "Where's the nozzle for the hoover? Where's the window cloth? WHAT HAVE YOU DONE WITH THE ANTIBAC?"

When Big Blue was returned to them, the good news from Halfords was that they could find nothing major wrong with her. They said that the diesel filter looked old, so the problem might simply have been a blockage, which fitted in with the sporadic loss of power. The new filter cost pennies and took only about an hour to fit. Phew!

An unexpected bonus of our trip to Halfords was that we hadn't realised that winter tyres have a direction of rotation. Halfords had fitted them for us last year but we had put them on ourselves this time – the wrong way round. It was not a problem for the short time that we had been using them, but had we not spotted our mishtayke, we learned that they could have shredded themselves...

In early January, we were supposed to be skiing in Italy, but besides car trouble, our Fidose had dealt us tenant trouble – and a robbery.

We were not too overwhelmed with distress about the delay to our departure. The newspapers reported that there was so much snow in the Alps that holiday makers were having to be helicoptered out of Zermatt. Most of the slopes in Monte Rosa had only just opened because the avalanche risk had been so far off the scale that it had taken until now to secure many of the pistes.

While Big Blue was being fixed, we had gone for a walk on the beach. At some point, playing with the pups, Mark's wallet had fallen out of his pocket.

Thankfully, someone found the wallet. Since it was still the season of goodwill to all men, our Good Samaritan kindly removed all £300 of our Christmas gift money and threw the wallet into the sea, along with all of Mark's bank and credit cards, his driving licence and his EHIC card. *(European Health Insurance Card.)*

We retraced our steps and fortunately found a rather soggy, sandy wallet near two metal detectorists. There was no-one else around. Just moments before, I had asked one of the detectorists if he'd found a wallet. "I haven't found anything." he told me sympathetically, before adding rather strangely "And neither has my mate!" I am only guessing, but today may have been his telepathic payday.

If his telepathy was working as well as I thought, I am sure that he would also know that I hoped beyond hope that he and his mate would choke on their ill-gotten gains and that Karma would find an appropriate reward for their utter disregard for somebody's valuables.

The irony was that we don't normally carry much cash. When you are on a budget and try to save a pound here and a pound there, it was crushing to lose so much money, especially since it had been given with love to help us on our way. It might even have helped to cover some of our fines! However, it was at least a blessing to have all the cards back. It would have been a fandangle of epic proportions to sort out replacing those just a couple of days prior to our already delayed departure for the Alps.

Well. That was the robbery. This was the tenant trouble.

Our tenants had given notice and moved out. Their prerogative, but it took us weeks to sort out all the damage to our flat. The second piece of my own advice that I had to swallow was that if you are renting property as a business, you can't be precious about it, even when it was once your treasured abode. However, I am still flabbergasted as to how people manage to be so destructive.

We had lived in the apartment for a decade without scraping a huge patch of varnish off the dining table, shattering five floor tiles and two wall tiles in the bathroom (tiles from a range now thankfully discontinued!); pulling off and losing a knob from the boiler that they never needed to touch; getting candle wax all over the carpet and furniture; pulling off and wrecking all of the blinds and smashing a glass shelf and two glass table tops.

It took me a full day to remove the grime from the bathroom and the oven, but the pièce de résistance was the tenant asking us what paint colours were on the walls. They reassured us that they had a parent who was a painter and decorator. We regained possession to find the walls daubed with random splodges of many shades to make good scratches, holes and marks; a dappled coat of many colours from several completely unrelated paint ranges.

Then they argued about the deposit!

42

HOW OUR RUN OF BAD LUCK ENDED

"Happy is he who forgets what can no longer be changed." –
Mark Twain

We did finally get to Italy to ski for the season. Our journey of 1000 miles back to Gressoney passed without incident – until the final 1.5 feet. Thwarted by a two-inch snow mound, it took us an hour and a half to get Big Blue up a slight but icy incline into the garage that belonged to our rental apartment.

In the process, we broke our snow chains and discovered that gripper tracks shoot forward at alarming speeds when turned upon by the drive wheel of a van on ice. We also discovered that tent pegs and a ski pole are insufficient to secure gripper tracks on ice. The tent pegs merely added the hazard of shrapnel to the gripper track ballistics and the ski pole bent itself irrecoverably into the sort of shape that you could achieve by trying to twist balloons into the likeness of a dachshund.

Once we did finally manage to get there, we had a wonderful season in the snow, thank you very much for asking. It was a legendary year for powder, although I won't bore you with details of glorious ski descents, adventures off piste and lots of woofy winter walks in golden sunshine.

Besides the obvious joys of being in a wintry wonderland, it was a delight to be back in our bubble; living our dreams remote from the real world of worry and conflict.

Well almost.

Communications from the police about the assault and the Planning Office about the boundary were a constant companion via email, although both assured us at every stage that everything was in hand. Then in mid-February, we got a phone call from the caravan storage company. They are lovely people, but I knew that it wasn't a social call. My heart sank.

"Hi! How are you?" they asked.

"Fine! How are you?" I replied.

"Fine," they concurred cheerily before dropping the bombshell. "Did you have a TV in your caravan?"

"Er, no – we've brought it with us to Italy. But if we had, am I right in thinking that we wouldn't have one now...?"

My powers of deduction really do rival those of Inspector Clouseau. "We have had a few break-ins, but your van seems to be OK. One man had his TV and £300 in cash taken from his van. Who leaves cash in their van?"

Who indeed? We weren't quick enough to think of that scam. Or the TV. Really, the Inland Revenue's confidence in our Master Criminal tendencies is utterly misplaced!

"The thieves disabled the CCTV, but it's fixed and improved. They forced your door lock, but it's all locked up again now."

So, there was nothing further to worry about.

Was there?!

43

THE CONCLUSION OF THE FIDOSE

"The law is an ass." - Mr Bumble in Charles Dickens' Oliver Twist.

The Boundary Dispute

"Land Grab from 95-year-old Widow Sanctioned by Local Council" was the gist of our campaign to fight for justice for Mark's Mum when her neighbour built his extension two feet over her boundary. But there, you see, no-one is interested.

For six months, the Council had assured us that everything was in hand. The neighbour had admitted to breaking the law by building without permission and the Council verified that "the building exceeds the original plans" and "appears to be on the neighbour's curtilage".

The Planning Officer recommended that enforcement action be taken. However, we wasted an hour of our lives watching the podcast of a meeting that would have taken ten minutes in the private sector. Vehement points were made in support of enforcement action being taken. Then they took a vote – and APPROVED the neighbour's retrospective plans. We were incredulous.

We fought the decision, of course.

The Planning Office told us that they couldn't get involved in boundary issues, since these were a matter for the civil courts. A little nugget that they shared with us only after the retrospective plans were approved, having spent the previous six months assuring us that everything was in hand.

The MP couldn't get involved in individual cases.

Mark's Mum was not upset enough for the Press. By not actually dying of shock, the story lacked a gripping emotional hook.

Consumer radio and TV programs thanked us for our interest but were not covering these subjects at this time.

A solicitor advised that boundary disputes are notoriously lengthy and difficult to solve. He needed £2000 up front for a consultation and professional survey – and that was just for starters. "The courts take a dim view of complaints made after the building is completed." he advised. Being 95, partially sighted, housebound and living alone with your son out of the country was, it seemed, insufficient mitigation.

Sometimes the best way to win is just to walk away. It was clearly a losing battle, so we swallowed hard, abandoned our sense of justice and opted to let the neighbour get away with it.

Luckily, Mark's cousin was able to nip over quickly one Sunday morning to supervise the fly-by-night erection of the new fence; clearly scheduled to take place while we were not around. As we suspected, the neighbour insisted that the new fence should be in line with his new extension, two feet over Mark's Mum's boundary. Thankfully, Mark's cousin successfully insisted that it should not.

The neighbour was less than contrite when Mark's cousin told him that he should be ashamed of himself for taking advantage of an elderly lady. But then, why should he be sorry? With property prices rising in the area, he had successfully flouted the law and made a small fortune.

So, let's raise a glass to our Public Bodies for their excellent work in protecting the elderly and vulnerable.

...

The Assault

The chap who launched an unprovoked attack on Mark was already known to the police. We had two independent witnesses to the incident and photographs to identify him, along with a photo of the actual bodily harm that he caused when he punched Mark in the face. His behaviour had been odd, so we were not surprised to find that he suffered from Asperger's Syndrome.

We told the Police that we hoped that he could get the help that he clearly needed. Nevertheless, whatever his problems, it was not OK to pull out a weapon and attack members of the public without warning – particularly the woman we found out that he'd knocked to the ground in similar circumstances. She had been too afraid to press charges.

Also, one day, he would pick on the wrong person and endanger himself.

Bringing him to justice should have been straightforward. Except that he prevaricated by not answering phone calls from the police and failing to turn up to interviews for which a 'competent adult' had to be found each time to accompany him. And so, by playing the system, the time frame for pressing charges elapsed and he walked away scot-free. So, he is out there folks and completely at liberty to do it again.

...

These incidents left us asking the question "Who does the law really protect?" Not the victim, it seems, if the perpetrator knows how to play the system.

However, before you lose faith in the Police and your Local Council completely, I can assure you that they are very, VERY efficient at collecting speeding fines!

*In no way do I wish to imply that our speeding fines were not just; technically, we had broken the law. The only point I wish to make here is that the weight of the law came swiftly and heavily down on us for very minor transgressions, like doing 70mph in a 70mph limit in a van, while the **really** guilty all got away scot free.*

SO, WHAT DID WE LEARN?

"The key to community is the acceptance, in fact the celebration of our individual and cultural differences. It is also the key to world peace." - M. Scott Peck

During our travels, we have been fortunate enough to meet and interact with many different nationalities. Perhaps one should not generalise, but as we discussed with Aleka and Florian in Český Krumlov, each nation does seem to have some of its own wonderful personality traits and stereotypes.

Purely as a bit of fun (so no letters please!) Mark compiled this list based on what the reaction would be from each nationality if they arrived at a café to find that the only free table is one chair short, but the other tables have chairs that are not in use.

...

In answer to the question "May I take this chair if no-one is using it?"

- **English** – "This is a British chair and only British arses may sit on it."
- **Scottish** – "Most of our chairs have already been taken by the English."
- **Welsh** – "Dim ond os byddwch yn gofyn yn garedig yn Gymraeg." *(Even though they were speaking English when you arrived.)*
- **Irish** – "We must retain neutrality on such matters."
- **French** – "Non."
- **Belgian** – "We have not yet properly determined that this is a chair."
- **Italian** – "I don't see why not, but I will let you know in two hours when I have finished lunch."
- **Dutch** – "First, you must pull up a chair and have a drink with us!"
- **German** – "Yes, but please take a cushion to make yourself more comfortable. And let me buy you a beer."
- **Austrian** – "Touch that chair at your peril."
- **Spanish** – "First we must decide on the fate of Gibraltar, then we talk about the chair."
- **Luxembourger** – "If you had arrived earlier, you could have had your own chair."
- **Portuguese** – "Why do you ask? Just take it!"
- **Swiss** – "It is our chair and we will keep it."
- **Greek** – "I can't believe that you don't have a chair. What is the world coming to?"
- **Norwegian** – "It is a dead chair."
- **Swedish** – "If you can drink this, then you can have the chair."
- **Icelandic** – "Can't you see that the little people are using the chair?"

- **Danish** – "If it will make you happy to have the chair, then of course."
- **Finn** – "Yes, but please take it quietly."
- **Russian** – "Does it look like someone is using it?"
- **Romanian** – "Yes, but I can show you where to find a more comfortable chair."
- **Polish** – "Our chair is your chair."
- **Slovenian** – "Yes, but first let me clean and polish the chair."
- **Hungarian** – "There was a time when we had much bigger chairs…"
- **Czech** – "It's not much of a chair, but sure!"
- **Croatian** – "First, tell me why you need the chair."
- **Turkish** – "Yes, but let me help you carry it."
- **Lithuanian** – "But what if I need it later?"
- **Latvian** – "Please do. I was worried that someone might sit there."
- **Estonian** – "Yes"
- **Slovak** – "The *PROBLEMS* I have had with that chair…"
- **American** – "You call that a chair? We have mice back home with bigger footstools."

"As long as you can laugh at yourself, you will never cease to be amused…" - Anon

EPILOGUE

With our apartment now vacant, we decided to move back in to enjoy the summer at home the following year, before departing on a trip around Spain and Portugal in September.

However, join us next time and discover how long we managed to stay 'in the brick' before we got itchy feet.

And then what happened when we set off south, but decided to turn left...

APPENDIX 1 - A POST TRIP PINT

A Barrel of Brewing Wisdom form a Former Beer Taster

As you found out when I was sold out by my husband to a German expert, a former profession of mine was as a beer taster in a brewery. One of the beers that we produced was Carlsberg, so it was the best job in the world. Probably...

In the same way that most people can't believe that a wee wifey can windsurf, most don't believe that I was a beer taster either – or that I gave it up! However, I can assure you that my beer-tasting skills are kept honed, although sadly, I no longer receive a beer allowance as part of my salary and warm English beer ('real ale') is tricky to come by on the Continent.

At least it means that I am properly qualified to have a look at that most important aspect of touring – a post-trip pint. Something that we look forward to with relish each time we return to the UK.

In fable, it is thought that Radegast, the Czech god of hospitality invented ale, although surprisingly, brewing is a bit of a feminine thing. In the past, brewing, like baking, was part of home-craft and the word 'Brewster' refers to a female brewer.

Radegast didn't file a patent, so a few fertility goddesses got in on the act and are also credited with the invention of ale. This makes sense – Beer Goggles have doubtless played a great part in human fertility over the millennia. Moving to fact from fable, there is 7000-year-old evidence that humans discovered a few good reasons to domesticate cereals – and one of these was the ability of wild yeast to spontaneously convert cereal sugars into alcohol.

Beer or Ale?

I deliberately talk about ale above, since 'ale' is the more generic term for an alcoholic beverage brewed from cereal. Ale can be flavoured with all kinds of things; honey, herbs, fruit – think of the Belgian Lambic beers. I have even heard of a recipe for Cock Ale. Guess how that is flavoured. (A chicken, alright. Unless Lorena Bobbitt had a side-line in brewing!)

What have the Romans ever done for us? Well, they gave us beer as we know it by introducing the hop plant to Britannia. Ale and beer are terms used interchangeably now, but to be correct, beer is simply ale flavoured with hops, or more correctly, with alpha acids derived from the female hop flower. (Those girls again!)

Beer is traditionally brewed from only four ingredients; water (known as 'liquor' in brewing terms – 'The Big Blue' in watersports terms), malt, hops and yeast. As Marco pointed out, the Germans take this seriously and their Purity Laws forbid the use of any other ingredients. However, some of the big breweries elsewhere have a tendency to pop in cheaper ingredients, like caramel for additional sugar, colour and flavour, or even sawdust, for that wonderful, wood-aged effect...

Each ingredient is critically important in the flavour. Breweries jealously guard their particular strain of yeast, often keeping their cultures locked away in a vault.

Malt is simply barley, which is partially germinated to convert its starches into sugars. These sugars are what the yeast then ferments into alcohol. Germination is stopped by roasting; the extent of the roasting can produce pale, blond malts right through to dark, almost burnt chocolate- and crystal malts, such as those which give Guinness its colour and character.

There are many types of hop, with vastly differing flavours and bitterness. Hops are 'mashed' (boiled up) with the malt and liquor. Mashing extracts the sugars from the malt and the flavour and bitterness from the hops to produce 'wort'. After mashing, the wort is cooled, the yeast added and fermentation takes place. Sometimes, 'aroma hops' are used at the very end of the process to 'dry hop' cask ales – a handful of aroma hops is simply dropped into the barrel before it is sealed.

Even the liquor is critically important; it is no accident that breweries proliferate in certain areas, such as Burton on Trent, where the chemical composition of the water is particularly suitable for brewing. Nowadays, geography is less important, as it is possible to treat or 'Burtonise' your liquor to ensure a great beer.

They say that Guinness is good for you. It is a little-known fact that in the Middle Ages, Nuns had a beer allowance of 8 pints per day. In days gone by, beer was actually safer to drink than water. The brewing process sterilises the water by boiling – and hops is credited with slightly antiseptic qualities.

Lager and Beer

A frequent question is "What is the difference between lager and beer?" The answer is partly process and partly species. The many strains of Saccharomyces Cerevisiae are ale yeasts, sometimes called 'top fermenting' yeasts, since they float to the top when fermentation is finished.

Saccharomyces Carlsbergensis is 'bottom fermenting' or lager yeast. You guessed – it floats to the bottom after fermentation. 'Lager' actually means 'to store' in German, so after fermentation, lager beers are stored over the yeast for a couple of weeks. This, in combination with the type of hops and blond malt used in brewing, gives that distinctive 'Continental' flavour.

Lager is then filtered, pasteurised and carbonated, so no live yeast remains once it is bottled or kegged. Lager is not, therefore, a 'live' product. Lager is served in a pub chilled and under a top pressure of sterile gas, so is easier to keep and has a longer shelf-life than a live beer. Lager is typically served very cold (4-7°C), so less of the flavour comes through. As beer tasters, we had to warm lager up in order to taste it properly. If you have ever picked up an old can at the end of a party, you will understand that a career in beer tasting can have its down sides, although at least we never found a fag-end in it...

German Weißbier 'White beer' is brewed with malted wheat rather than barley. It is fermented with ale yeast and is generally left unfiltered, retaining its cloudy, white haze of suspended 'Hefe – yeast'.

Beers are not stored or 'lagered' after fermentation, but can be filtered, gassed and pasteurised in the same way to make them keep for longer. The proliferation of these 'chilled and filtered' keg beers (otherwise known as 'sacrilege'!) led to the formation of CAMRA – the Campaign for Real Ale.

'Live' beers or 'Real Ales' are racked off from under the yeast following fermentation, put in a barrel, 'finings' added to clear the beer, dry hopped if necessary – and are ready to drink! To be stored and served correctly, these live beers require good cellar-craft, as they still contain some yeast (which continues to ferment to give the slight sparkle = 'cask conditioned'.) They are not over-chilled and are pumped by hand under atmospheric pressure rather than sterile gas. Real ales thus have a short shelf-life and certainly last only a few days once the barrel has been 'tapped', or opened, as this allows air in. The flavour is more intense in beer than lager partly because of the ingredients and partly because beer is served warmer, at cellar temperature of around 12-14°C.

While beer barrels are no longer made of wood, measurements for beer remain gloriously imperial. A Barrel is 36 gallons, which is 4 Firkins, 8 Pins, 2 Kilderkins – or $^2/_3$ of a Hogshead. 2 Hogsheads is a Butt and, if you are ever told your Butt looks big, you can always riposte that it is only half a Tun!

So, there you have it. If you haven't got a Grand Tour to talk about next time you have a pint, you can tell your mates some Firkin facts and how beer is a girl thing.

Jackie 'Firkin' L

APPENDIX 2 - TIPS FOR PLANNING THE PERFECT TRIP

"Choose an arbitrary purpose and stick to it!" – *Tony Wilson*

The meaning of life was never clear to me until I read this quote from the late Tony Wilson. TV Reporter, founder of Factory Records and The Hacienda nightclub in Manchester, Tony Wilson was played by Steve Coogan in the excellent film about his life, '24-Hour Party People'.

An arbitrary purpose is also worth keeping in mind when you are planning your travels. "So much world. So little time!" is the perennial problem faced by anyone planning a tour – so how do you narrow down a WHOLE WORLD of experience into something manageable?

Well here, let me help.

I. TIME

Time and tide wait for no man." – *Chaucer, Shakespeare –*
and Anon!

A traveller always wants more time. Time is a scarce commodity, so spend it well.

In times past, our trip planning was simple; fit the largest number of far-flung adventures into 2-week slices of leave from work. Although we have abandoned the world of work, family and other commitments do mean that we pop back to Blighty every now and again to visit those we love. So even for us, travel time is limited.

Clearly, time dictates how far afield you can realistically get on one trip.

My advice on this is not to be too ambitious. Don't try to pack in too much, otherwise your trip will be all about driving past lots of roses, but never enjoying their beauty or their scent and missing out on everything else that lives and grows in fields of roses.

1. TRAVELLERS' TOOLS

"Maps codify the miracle of existence." - Nicholas Crane in the book 'Mercator: The Man Who Mapped the Planet'

Poring over a map is one of the best ways of tailoring your route exactly as you want it, with diversions and excursions to whatever points of interest may attract you along the way.

These days, of course, online route planning makes things considerably easier, with detailed routes illustrated at the mere click of a button.

We have found Scribble Maps to be an invaluable online resource. Not only can you plan where to go, you can mark potential campsites and places of interest (with added notes!) on your own personalised route maps.

But we still haven't decided on WHERE TO GO?

1. WHERE TO GO?!

I haven't been everywhere, but it's on my list." – Susan Sontag

If you want to know how to make the most of the time that you have, here, I share some of the ruses that we employ in planning our trips;

1. Choose a Theme

"I stand upon my desk to remind myself that we must constantly look at things in a different way." – John Keating (Robin Williams) in the film 'Dead Poets Society'

We find themes a very useful way to plan our travels.

- We were married in a lighthouse. Lighthouses are always marked on maps and are, by their nature, often in very beautiful places. So, we often visit lighthouses.
- We are interested in history, so we are drawn to castles as well as battlefields and historic monuments.
- Having read my blog 'The Knowledge – Toilet Training', my friend bought me 'A Spotter's Guide to Toilets', and told me that it was not Christmas present, but a mission...
- But if you are not into anything as trite as toilets, there is always good old UNESCO, who has done a fair bit of leg work in identifying and listing some the world's most fabulous places!
- The website Touropia is also a great starting

point, as it lists the Top Ten things to see in each
country.

- We are windsurfers, so "The Kite and Windsurf Guide to Europe" has a significant part to play in our travel planning...

- Our surname, Lambert, is unremarkable. However, Lambert's Oaks is a house in Surrey that gave its name to the famous horse race, The Oaks. Lambert's Castle is an Iron Age hill fort in Dorset (and a fortress in New Jersey!); There is a Lambert Bay in the British Virgin Islands and another near Cape Town. If you fly into St Louis, you will land at Lambert International Airport and if you sit with a glass of wine in the centre of Verona in Italy, you may be shaded by the tallest tower in Verona; the 84m high Torre dei Lamberti.

Can you see where I am going with this? Even if you're not into serious family history, you can have a bit of fun and find some interesting places along the way.

B. Classic Routes

"The Grand Tour is just the inspired man's way of heading home." – Paul Theroux

Everyone has heard of Route 66. It is THE archetypal American Road Trip – the 3,945km Main Street of America from Chicago to LA.

But you don't have to cross The Pond to find Classic Routes. There are plenty of well-established routes that you can follow closer to home.

- Germany is particularly good at themed routes. A couple which were on our radar were the Castle Road (Burgenstraße) – a 1000km (600m) route taking in some of the best castles you are ever likely to see. Established in 1954, the Castle Road now extends as far as Prague in the Czech Republic. (If you're brave – you can do the whole thing on a bicycle.)
- There is also Southern Germany's Romantic Road (Romantische Straße) – a 350km route from the River Main to the Alps, which winds through the picturesque forests and mountains of Bavaria.
- However, if you're into asparagus, cheese, glass, half-timbered houses – or what about BEER or wine? Germany boasts over 80 such Themed Routes.
- The European Route of Industrial Heritage is more interesting that you might think. How about a Zeppelin museum? The ERIH website is very straightforward and can be searched by theme, country or region.
- Or, you can always just think about what interests you and plan your own!

C. Recommendations from Locals or Other Travellers

"Travelling is like flirting with life. It's like saying, 'I would stay and love you, but I have to go; this is my station.'" – Lisa St. Aubin de Teran

This is a planning tool not to be overlooked. Our fabulous white-water rafting trip to Colorado, which included a first descent of Red Rock Canyon (where Butch & Sundance jumped in the film) came about solely because of a chance conversation with a Whitewater Rafting Guide in Costa Rica on our Honeymoon. You really cannot beat taking advantage of the first-hand experiences of a like-minded traveller.

One of the reasons that Mark and I are keen to learn languages is that an unfailing pathway to travel joy is chatting to locals. If you want to find that secluded beach, that amazing restaurant or the finest vineyard in the area, there is no-one better to tell you about it than a proud and friendly local who knows the area like the back of their hand.

D. Go Where No-one Has Gone Before

"Bizarre travel plans are dancing lessons from God." – Kurt Vonnegut

Mark and I are not fans of crowds, so given the choice, we will always follow the road less travelled. In our first year of touring with the caravan, we discovered many of the 'boring bits' in between the well-known tourist destinations in France were AMAZING. And not only that, we had them all to ourselves.

We once planned a 2-week holiday around an Umbrella Museum in Gignese, Italy that we had read about in our Italian Language Textbook. Well, it just had to be done!

This rather unscientific approach to planning has led us to some amazing experiences, such as a back-street Carnival club in Rio. In Italy, we stumbled upon a spectacular International Music Festival in Stresa (near the Umbrella Museum) and got the last two tickets. Our hostess in Barolo force-fed us with fresh, hand-gathered truffles (she was incredulous that we had never tasted truffles with eggs for breakfast and sought to complete our lives!) Then, in Tuscany, we watched the sun set from the terrace of our own mini-castle eating a plate of succulent, fresh figs with a bottle of fine, red wine that tasted of rubies and Italian sunshine.

Had we had a plan, none of this would have happened. Doing the odd will bring about adventures that you never expected.

E. I've Always Wanted To...

"Twenty years from now you will be more disappointed by the things that you didn't do than by the ones you did do." –
Mark Twain
"So, throw off the bowlines. Sail away from the safe harbour. Catch the trade winds in your sails. Explore. Dream. Discover." (Still Mark Twain.)
"Experiences are something that you will never regret!" (Me!)

F. Subject to Change Without Notice...

"A good traveller has no fixed plans and is not intent on arriving."
– Lao Tzu

In the world of work, things are rigid and proscribed. We were terrorised by time and ruled by the epithet P.P.P.P – Proper Planning Prevents Poor Performance.

My best advice for travelling is don't overdo the planning and don't try to fit in too much. The joy of travel is discovery and you never know what you will find on the way.

Also, be free to change your plans based on weather, recommendations or simply a flight of fancy. Carpe Diem – Seize the Day. It will make your travels extraordinary!

G. Don't Discount your Doorstep

"You can spend your whole life travelling around the world searching for the Garden of Eden, or you can create it in your backyard." - Khang Kijarro Nguyen

I can't believe that I saw New Zealand before I visited Scotland. So often, we overlook what is right on our doorstep.

Britain is a beautiful country. Truthfully, in all of my travels around the world, I have not found anywhere that comes close to the variety of landscapes, culture and history crammed into so compact an area. We just take it for granted because it is familiar.

While I have set foot on six of the seven continents, my favourite view IN THE WORLD is still the magnificent 360-degree panorama from the top of Hengistbury Head near Christchurch in Dorset.

For further British Travel Ideas, check out the Visit Britain website.

I. WHERE TO STAY?

"We're a provider of experiences, not strictly accommodation..." – Nathan Blecharczyk, founder of Airbnb

There are plenty of groups which list approved and inspected campsites. For UK adventures, we are members of both the Camping and Caravanning Club and Caravan and Motorhome Club.

In Europe, we use ACSI, which lists, rates and offers reviews of nearly 10,000 campsites, giving clear details of the facilities available at each one. The associated ACSI Camping Card offers off-season discounts.

We rarely book campsites. This gives us flexibility to

change our plans if we choose, or move on if, in spite of our careful research, we don't like the look of things when we get there. (This has happened a couple of times.)

However, in peak times, in popular places – or if it's a very long way to the next campsite – booking is probably worthwhile.

WARNING

"We shall not cease from exploration and the end of all our exploring will be to arrive where we started and know the place for the first time." – T. S. Eliot

We were planning to tour in our caravan for a couple of years, but the more you see, the more you see that, well, there is always more to see!

Be warned. Travel is highly addictive. If you ever think that you're a travel addict on the road to recovery think again. The only road that you're likely to be on is the one to your next adventure.

We had intended to tour in the caravan for three years. At the last count, Mark had 16 years of trips planned out.

And even then, we won't have finished Europe.

ACKNOWLEDGEMENTS

I would like to thank the following people who have helped me more than they can know.

Joan and Jim Dinsdale – my Mum and Dad, for unconditional love, nurturing my appreciation of wild nature and their unfailing confidence that I could achieve anything at all.

Kath Livingstone – the puppies' 'Ant Kath', who thinks of everyone before herself and is quite simply the kindest and most selfless person that I have ever met.

Helen and Bernie McClean – for inspiration and on numerous occasions, putting up a homeless pair of vagabonds with four dogs without batting an eyelid!

Debbie Purse – at Book Covers for You who has once again brought to life exactly what was in my head.

Sophie Wallace – @SophieWallaceProofreading for her painstaking attention to detail and excellent advice on publishing.

To My Readers Around the World - to all the wonderful people who have bought both this and my previous book.

THANK YOU! Your kind words, reviews and support mean everything.

And of course, Mark, Kai, Rosie, Ruby and Lani who never fail to light up my day.

ABOUT THE AUTHOR

Jackie Lambert has long had a passion for travel and adventure. Always a bit of a tomboy, it was an accidental whitewater rafting trip down the Zambezi that really opened her eyes to the experiences that the world has to offer. The trip was not, as she expected, 'floating down the river looking at wildlife.' Somewhere between the adrenaline of tackling Grade 5 rapids in crocodile-infested waters and the raw beauty of sleeping under the stars on the banks of the river, she determined that she was no longer content to live her life in thin slices.

Since then, she has travelled as much as time and budget would allow and has rafted major rivers on every continent except Antarctica. Before meeting her husband, Mark, she took a sabbatical from work (although she was single at the time, she asked for - and was granted - "maternity leave"!) to spend several months backpacking around Fiji, Australia and New Zealand.

A keen skier and windsurfer, Jackie is a Team Rider for the UK's National Watersports Festival, to which she has contributed many articles and blogs about windsurfing. She is also the wordsmith behind her own dog-centric caravan travel blog, World Wide Walkies, which has been featured in the Eurotunnel Le Shuttle Newsletter, Dog Friendly Magazine and other doggie travel blogs around the world.

She and Mark were made redundant in 2016 – and have been travelling ever since.

Facebook: @JacquelineLambertAuthor

Amazon: www.amazon.com/author/jacquelinelambert

DOG BLESS YOU ALL

Don't forget to leave a review to help other readers.
What did you think of my book? Who do you think might enjoy it? Which bit was your favourite? How did it make you feel? Or anything else!
Your feedback is very much appreciated.

Milton Keynes UK
Ingram Content Group UK Ltd.
UKHW041507311023
431669UK00005B/395